Coping With
Study Strategies

by
Gary Bergreen

THE ROSEN PUBLISHING GROUP, INC.
New York

*This book is dedicated to
my wife, Juanita, and
to my children,
Jason, Eric, and Susan*

Published in 1986, 1990 by The Rosen Publishing Group, Inc.
29 East 21st Street, New York, N Y 10010

Copyright 1986, 1990 by Gary Bergreen   91-17740

REVISED EDITION 1990

Manufactured in the United States of America.

Library of Congress Cataloging-In-Publication Data

Bergreen, Gary.
        Coping with study strategies.   52518

        (Coping)
        Bibliography: p.
        Includes index.
        1. Study. Method of.   I. Title.   II. Series.
LB1049.B42   1986   371.3′028′12   86-3252
ISBN 0-8239-1140-3

About the Author

GARY BERGREEN has taught in the southern California area for the past fourteen years. He has taught various speech communication and management coursework at Chaffey College, in Alta Loma, and also many drama and communicative skills courses at the secondary levels in the Corona, Riverside area. He has also designed a number of language arts activities and classroom-oriented workshops for teachers.

After graduating from Utah State, he completed work at the graduate level and was granted a Master of Arts degree in Speech Communication from California State University at Long Beach. Here, he also obtained his secondary and community college teaching credentials. He has extensive academic background in Communicative Disorders and in Computer Sciences, both with a diverse emphasis on communicative procedures. He has written many book reviews for newspapers as well.

THEN SAID A TEACHER, SPEAK TO US OF TEACHING

And he said:
No man can reveal to you aught but which already lies
half asleep in the dawning of your knowledge.

The teacher who walks in the shadow of the temple, among
his followers, gives not of his wisdom but rather of
your own mind.

The astronomer may speak to you of his understanding of
the regions of weight and measure, but he cannot
conduct you thither.

The musician may sing to you of the rhythm which is in all
space, but he cannot give you the ear which arrests the
rhythm nor the voice that echoes it.

And even as each one of you stands alone in God's knowledge,
so much each one of you be alone in his knowledge of God
and in his understanding of the earth.

Kahlil Gibran

Table of Contents

CHAPTER I

Learning to Learn

THOUGHT: ...and with all thy getting get understanding
Proverbs 4:7

"I just can't remember" are words that have echoed inside many a student's head during examinations, quizzes, and oral recitations. "Where did I go wrong?" is another question of the ages, signalling the beginnings of frustration and failure as students become overwhelmed by the demands of their education. But this need not be the case for most of us. Learning can be an enjoyable, lifelong endeavor, a personal challenge to overcome poor study habits and to replace them with new ones. Regardless of how old you are, or how educated you may be, there is still a future full of surprises, new skills and knowledge, exciting possibilities.

The art of learning is one that takes motivation, planning, concentration and sound reasoning. Add to that the key elements in STUDY STRATEGY: open-mindedness, making learning meaningful, the desire to practice and improve your retention, and learning how to learn; all are your stepping-stones to success.

Open-Mindedness

According to John Dewey, open-mindedness includes "an active desire to listen to more sides than one; to give heed to facts from whatever source they come; to give full attention to alternative possibilities; to recognize the possibility of error even in those beliefs that are dearest to us." Uninhibited in this way, we must actively learn what we need to know. Develop a 'need to know' attitude and you will automatically increase the rate and degree of learning. In the beginning, then, our main focus for improving our study habits is on keeping the mind free and clear of any distractions.

1

Meaningful Learning

Old learning is often the basis for new learning. But we must use our thinking abilities to connect their relationships. By using your concentration powers, creating the right atmosphere, and developing positive, self-satisfying feelings about what you learn, your study efforts will quickly yield many beneficial rewards.

Heuristic is a word that means literally finding out, and this method of learning has been described as the method of causing you to discover things for yourself. In fact, it throws the entire responsibility not on the teacher but exclusively on you as the learner. Here you must decide what your goals and learning tasks must be. So, as we develop our study strategy, let's learn to identify a clear (attainable) learning objective. Once we do, little time will be wasted and we will know what goals we are striving toward. Next, we will want to devise a study schedule so that we can plan ahead, giving us enough time to learn what is assigned. And then we need to critically think through our learning tasks step by step as we decide on a deadline for achieving our goals. This all sounds easy enough. But remember, in this method of STUDY STRATEGY, there is no one else around to prod you. Thus, your desire to learn must come from within.

How do I know what to look for? you may ask. Well, begin by looking at the vehicle of learning-language. At the core of deciphering units of meaning we must orient ourselves to the ways our language can help us. Specifically, we learn by understanding sentences and utterances, which can be classified in the following way:

1. INFORMATIVE STATEMENTS are often used by authors and teachers simply to report information or revise our thinking about misinformation. Example: ''Your car is parked in the Principal's parking space'' may be very meaningful to you.

2. INTERROGATIVE STATEMENTS provide us with the unique ability to inquire about information. ''When is this assignment due?'' is an example.

3. DIRECTIVE STATEMENTS give us the necessary avenues for obtaining specific directions. Here, the primary function is to shape or elicit a desired response from you.

4. EXPRESSIVE STATEMENTS do not always inform others. Instead, they may be used to vent emotions. Often, no audience is required, as when you hit your finger with a hammer and loudly shout "Ouch!" or "Son of a gun!"

Such statements are all designed to influence you in some way. The more extensive the sentence or utterance, the more likely it is to perform more than one of these four functions.

Practice

Practice learning little by little, integrating each new idea into meaningful units that eventually help you to understand the whole picture, or the subject under scrutiny. The realization that you have discovered new, more meaningful knowledge will unfold as you systematically put your mental energies to work. Practice what you learn intently and continually at the beginning of your learning experiences. Review your learning experiences often. Divide and conquer them until they become second nature to you; retain what you learn in this way and you will have developed a powerful study skill..

Concentration

The power to concentrate is one of your greatest challenges and will be a very valuable learning tool. It is an ability that many students lack. It requires a good deal of effort to shut out distractions, physical ones such as fatigue and hunger, and outside distractions such as street noises and friendly chatting. Obviously, most of these distractions activate (and aggravate) our senses: sight, sound, touch, taste, and smell. With just a little effort, we can eliminate distractions simply by ignoring them.

Furthermore, you can increase your powers of concentration by (1) actively developing your study habits, (2) learning to use your time more effectively, (3) becoming involved with the learning task quickly. So, abandon your fears and self-doubts concerning your ability to learn. Everyone can learn! For some it may take a little more time and patience. But as your concentration improves and your desire to develop new abilities into a workable STUDY

STRATEGY increases, you will be quite surprised at how much more easily new knowledge will fall into place.

You need not feel that you are completely alone in your endeavors to learn. There are teachers, friends, school and public librarians, and many other learning center counselors and instructors to guide you toward the vast resources of books, self-teaching programs, and a variety of learning facilities with which you will want to become acquainted. But, in this quest for understanding, one of the most important things you learn is not just where to find the right answers at the right time. Rather, your most valuable lesson is learning how to learn and enjoying it more.

A brilliant scientist by the name of Karl Pearson explains in his book *The Grammar of Science:*

"I have recollection of at least 90 percent of the facts that were taught me in school; but the notion of method which I derived from my instructor in Greek Grammar (the contents of which I have long since forgotten) remains in my mind as the valuable part of school equipment."

Making Sense

Making sense has been characterized as relating events in the real world to our own past experiences, our expectations, and in short, our cognitive abilities. We do not learn by chance. Learning is the result of our conscious experiences, and it is best facilitated when those experiences are deliberately and systematically sought by the learner.

Critical Thinking

The English philosopher John Locke was of the opinion that two men must come to the same conclusion on a given subject if the following conditions are observed: (1) these men must have all the evidence or circumstances of the case under scrutiny; (2) they must be free from bias; (3) they must give their minds seriously to the subject. On the surface this sounds fairly straightforward. However, there are other implications to the complex inner workings of our thought processes. Thorough research, of course, is needed when we are investigating any topic. Yet, the organization of data and the way each bit of information is perceived is often a very subjective matter. It is important to use some criteria or standards of judgment when critically looking into any subject matter. So, when you study an assignment look not only for a particular point of view, but also determine how the information was analyzed and interpreted. This will help you distinguish facts from myths, fantasy from what is valid and reliable in the real world.

Critical thinking is based upon evaluative tools that help us place our new knowledge in some orderly perspective. Study your assignments critically, looking for terms that are defined clearly and concisely. And as you reflect upon them try to question, summarize, and redefine new concepts and ideas. Then integrate the new with the old information you already have, building concept upon concept as you learn new skills and become acquainted with new subjects in education.

Why Some Students Don't Study More

There are probably as many reasons why students don't study as there are students who drop out of school without graduating and lose their chances for a successful future. Here are only four of the most common reasons:

1. They fail to realize the importance of studying.
2. They believe that an education is not very valuable.
3. They have a defeatist attitude.
4. They feel that what they learn will soon become old and outdated, and so why study in the first place?

Why Some People Enjoy Learning

Being too lazy to complete a homework assignment is generally considered a sign of inability to learn a certain subject. But the majority of students today are not lazy. While we all don't fit into the genius category and are not always at the top of the class in grades, most of us find a variety of subjects worth exploring. In fact, you may know some students who fall asleep in Biology or History but are wide awake and actively take part in discussion in Science, Mathematics, or English.

Because each person matures at a slightly different rate or age level, it is not uncommon to see someone who you thought would never make it through the school year turn around and become a serious student and graduate with honors. Such a person is often referred to as a 'late bloomer.' That is a person who has finally reached a maturation level that allows him to grow in learning, finding the relevancy of studying in an effort to gain an education that will take him on toward attaining other personal goals.

You probably know of many other students who really have a 'head for facts' or a 'thirst for new knowledge.' You might find them reading far into the night because they have been absorbed in the ideas of an author. These students have developed a curious nature that leads them further into new fields of endeavor, learning more and more about career-related matters, learning new skills and discovering fascinating hobbies and gaining knowledge in general. Many of your friends who appear to have very few daily problems may have searched through literature to discover important ways of coping.

There are as many reasons for students to enjoy studying as there are students who graduate and find doors opening to them in many fields. The point is that you must decide what kind of student you want to be. If you are serious about furthering your education, you must next examine your motives. After that, developing a study strategy to get you to where you want to go will be easy.

So, let's stop here and consider some important reasons why you should get started on a study plan:

1. I need to learn to get ahead in the future.
2. I need to learn more in less time.
3. I need to replace feelings of frustration with self-satisfaction.
4. I need to expand my horizons.
5. I need to learn how to learn.

Well, now it's up to you. What four reasons will motivate you to learn to study better? Give it some thought and then write those reasons down for future reference:

I want to study more effectively because:
Better study habits will help me _____
Better study habits will help me _____
Better study habits will help me _____
Better study habits will help me _____

That's a start. Keep a positive attitude and a sincere willingness to learn. Those are the keys that will help you unlock doors to the processing centers of your brain where new knowledge will be recorded and stored.

So, what do I do to get started on improving my study skills? Good question! Begin by getting mentally and physically ready. DO THIS FIRST:

Ready-Steady-Study!

• Find a quiet room with a chair, a desk, and lots of light.
• Get a pencil, eraser, and plenty of paper.
• Have a dictionary handy.
• Now, put your assignments in front of you in the order you need to complete them (by dates they are due).

NOT BAD! You have completed the first step in STUDY STRATEGY—painlessly. So, get comfortable and just relax for one minute. You deserve it.

Now, step two is just as easy—take a deep breath and let's take a quick look at your first assignment. Find the directions. Read them over two or three times. BE PATIENT IF YOU DON'T UNDERSTAND THEM THE FIRST TIME. Look for examples and work through those. Check your class notes for any special instructions. Concentrate on organizing your thoughts before you start the assignment. Know the purpose of the assignment, as well as what it is asking you to do, and have a good idea of what your completed work should look like. With that mental map to guide you, let's get ready to continue.

Now Is No Time to Get Discouraged and Quit

During your early years in school, you may have developed a trial-and-error approach to doing school work. Because you did not have a study plan, many of your assignments probably got lost or were done incorrectly or not at all. You became confused or frustrated, so you gave up. From there it was easy to put the entire responsibility for learning on the teacher rather than on yourself. The results: poor study habits plus a poor general attitude toward school. You may have even fallen into one or more of the following pitfalls: (1) a bad method of learning that you mastered only too well; (2) the wrong subject at an abnormally high level of difficulty that you muddled through only too well; and (3) misinformation that you were required to memorize, which you did only too well.

Well, it's time to turn things around. No overnight miracles here! But with a little practice on improving your study skills you will eventually get through more of your assignments with ease. Take stock of those poor learning skills you may have right now, and let's work on replacing them with a better STUDY STRATEGY.

Study Warm-Ups

Have you ever said to yourself, ''I just can't settle down and get to work on my assignments?'' The time is not right, the moon is full, my car is calling me, it needs my immediate attention, or some other equally earth-shaking revelation makes it impossible for you to take pencil, paper, and assignment seriously in hand. Well, here is the answer to all of that.

The STUDY WARM-UPS throughout this book should be attempted when you need an incentive to get the job done. They are designed to challenge your mental abilities and are fun to work at. Use one to help you develop a more positive approach in those first few minutes of your study session. Practice using your power of concentration, your ability to read and follow directions, and work through these activities as a springboard to your other assignments. You will eventually want to modify some to go along with your school work.

Awareness Counts!

1. Look around the room. Pay special attention to small details for about one minute.
2. Next, close your eyes and mentally name as many objects as you can recall.
3. At the same time, using a pencil and scratch pad, make a mark for each time you named some remembered object. This will be your awareness count.
4. Open your eyes and look around the room a second time. What objects did you miss?
5. Finally, close your eyes and try again. Top your awareness score by trying once again to name any other objects you observed in the room. See all of them clearly in your 'mind's eye' as you did before.

This one too easy for you? Then try using a stopwatch or kitchen timer to put a little pressure on yourself. Complete each of the above steps in thirty-second intervals. You will be surprised at how quickly you can sharpen your powers of concentration with this activity. And of course, improving your ability to remember things will help you retain what you need for that next assignment.

Begin here. Write down your time and your score:

Time Starting:____Stopping:____Score:____
Time Starting:____Stopping:____Score:____
Time Starting:____Stopping:____Score:____

The "TH" Brain Teaser

1. Write down as many words as possible that begin with the letters "th."
2. Each "th" word may appear on your list only once.
   O.K.: there, their, and they're.
   Not O.K.: thirty, thirty-one, thirty-two.
3. You may look around your immediate environment for 'inspiration.' But you may not look in books or dictionaries for help. In other words, the "th" words must come directly from your own brain power.

You will probably want to use other letter combinations for this STUDY WARM-UP. Try *ch, ph, sh, cl, cr, cy.*

YOUR SCORE

1-10 =	"The pits"
11-20 =	"A mental mongoose"
21-20 =	"A nimble thinker"
31-40 =	"A stupifier"
41-50 =	"Genuine genius"
51-60 =	"Thingamoabod guru"
60 + =	"Master of the art"

Daphee-Nishuns

Make up nonsense definitions for each of the following:

1. Bettle-Bomb _____
2. Muck-a-Luck _____
3. Shoebedoo _____
4. Razamataz _____
5. Ram-a-Lamb _____
6. Umpa-Lumpa _____
7. Ohm-o-Way _____
8. Rudy-Toot-Toot _____
9. Monkey-Shine _____
10. Whackadoo _____

Now, it's your turn. Go ahead. Make up five nonsense words of your own and then give them equally ridiculous definitions.

A)_____   _____
B)_____   _____
C)_____   _____
D)_____   _____
E)_____   _____

Finally, use a dictionary to find two very 'strange' words, ones you think are particularly unusual. Write down the words and their definitions:

A)_____   _____

B)_____   _____

Revealing Concealing Words

1. Write down a fairly long word such as *concentration* or *communication*.
2. Now, see how many words you can find using just the letters in that word.

   Example 1: Concentration
              cent
              at
              on

   Example 2: Communication
              coat
3. You may use the letters as often as they appear in the original word. Don't cross them off, though. You will want to use them again and again as you write down new words.

Try this STUDY WARM-UP with your vocabulary words. Practice this one daily to increase your word power. You will soon find that those spelling words that gave you so much difficulty are an enjoyable challenge.

Origami Swami

1. Place three pieces of paper and a pencil on the desk in front of you.
2. Take one piece of paper and fold it into a paper airplane.
3. Now, take your pencil and write down, step by step, the directions for someone else to duplicate your folded work of art. Include specific instructions and diagrams for reproducing your origami.

4. Use the directions you wrote down to make an exact copy of your paper object. Did it come out the same?
5. Give your directions to someone and see if he can follow each step to make an origami exactly like your masterpiece.
6. Finally, set your origami in front of you and write a one-page story about it. Use your imagination. Have some fun. Don't worry about spelling or punctuation. Just write ideas on your paper and see what happens. Make a few doodles and sketches in the margins to depict your ideas and your origami.

Origami is defined by *Webster's New World Dictionary* as ''a traditional Japanese art of folding paper to form flowers, animal figures, etc.'' The library has many interesting books showing how to make a variety of objects.

CHAPTER II

Sharpening Your Learning Skills

THOUGHT: As turning the logs will make a dull fire burn,
so change of studies a dull brain.
H.W. Longfellow

Do you know what to listen for? Listen carefully when you are given directions for an assignment. Learn to visualize each step and how one is related to the other. Listen, concentrate, and work through the examples both while and after your teachers explain them. Tune in to what is being asked—understand the assignment BEFORE you begin. Find out (1) what the purpose is; (2) how to follow directions to arrive at the expected answers; (3) what those answers should look like once you have completed the assignment; and (4) how much time you will need to finish.

Learn by Listening

"You're not listening!" How many times have you heard that? Too many? Well then, listen to this: Good listening skill is one of the important skills you can learn easily, one that you will use constantly as you study and learn. In fact, almost 70 percent of our day is spent in gaining and sorting out information. Yet, we really pay attention only to messages that are of real interest to us, ignoring those that seem dull or unimportant. Furthermore, you may think that you are listening when you're not! Hearing someone say something and listening to someone give instructions are not the same. We continually hear sounds, 100 percent of the time. We cannot simply push a button to turn our hearing off and on. But listening, that's another matter! Here, we become actively involved by concentrating on what is being said, by taking notes, and by remembering important information. If we have taken the responsibility and have done our part in this learning process, those questions on tests and homework assignments become less of a problem. Here, the brain has also become actively involved by processing details for us to recall at the appropriate time. When we take a passive role, the brain tends to take the day off. The processing becomes sluggish and we lose valuable time and energy with little to show for it.

In summary then, LEARN TO LISTEN ACTIVELY FOR IMPORTANT DIRECTIONS AND DETAILS.

Clarifying Details

Listen to clues that a teacher uses during lectures. There are certain key words that those straight "A" students have learned early on to identify. Be especially alert to these five terms that teachers use in giving assignments:

DEFINITION: This word will signal you to write and speak in specific terms. The teacher wants you to limit whatever topic is assigned or under discussion. So listen and write down all definitions in the lecture.

COMPARISONS: When your teacher explains theories and concepts by showing the similarities and differences between them, chances are you will be expected to do the same.

DRAWINGS: Often, sketches and diagrams that the teacher draws for you on the blackboard help you visualize what is important. Copy all drawings for later reference.

POINTING: Teachers have a way of 'pointing' out what is important to remember, especially on a test. They literally point to statements in the textbook, or they may verbally point to them by saying something like, "Now, remember this..." or "The main thing to keep in mind is..." So, be alert when you hear these and similar 'pointing phrases.'

ILLUSTRATIONS: These may include a variety of examples to which you need to pay attention in order to understand the concept being discussed. A teacher may explain a major idea by telling a story that parallels the ideas being discussed. Find the parallel points by taking notes.

It is easy to get lost or at least confused during some lectures. So, listen for those key words and phrases, then write down what is being said; if you are still not sure of what you heard, ask a question. This will at the very least slow the discussion down to help you catch up; at the most you will have taken an active part in learning, which in turn will help you remember more. In this way, your assignments will be a lot easier to handle. Remember, don't let those directions and ideas frustrate you needlessly. Always stay one jump ahead!

Once you understand your assignment, put yourself on a 'need to know' basis, organize your time accordingly, and concentrate diligently on your work. Shut out all noise and distractions. In short, settle into your study session by paying close attention to what you are to learn. Some of your assignments will demand that you make clear and accurate decisions. Learn to think like a detective, a coach, or an umpire. Get all the facts straight first, and then with a little self-confidence and determination make your judgment call. Use sound reasoning to come to well-thought-out decisions by sharpening your powers of observation and concentration. Exercise your brain—observe those little details that you have overlooked before: important dates, formulas, lists of items, places, and names. Condition yourself to find those same details in your study sessions. Seek a more intelligent point of view. Look for the unique angles in familiar topics. Practice sharpening your powers of observation throughout the day as well as when doing class assignments.

Skimming Your Assignments

Some students (but not many, thank goodness) count the number of pages first to see just how difficult their assignment is going to be. But, of course, you are not one of those students. So, here is a better way to begin your study sessions. Forget about the length of your assignment. Skim rapidly through and find the important details. Locate the material that looks easy and the sections that may give you some trouble. Now, develop the habit of breaking your study time and those assignment sections into smaller, more convenient units. DIVIDE AND CONQUER! As you skim quickly through your work, make some mental notes that will remind you where to find those words that are printed in italics or boldface. They are often the answer to your chapter questions, and they often show up on examinations. As you skim, also take time to examine the graphs, pictures, charts, and diagrams. Read the chapter summary and questions BEFORE you go back to read the chapter or do the assignment. As you improve your skimming strategy, you will become more aware of the author's use of verbal and visual road signs, pointing out what he thinks is of most importance in relation to the chapter's subject.

So, follow this verbal map, as you skim, and notice the landmarks indicated by subtopics and main headings. The more information the author includes on one particular subtopic, the more important it is for you to read it slowly. On the other hand, if little space is devoted to a subtopic, the author may have felt that it was interesting but not too significant.

Now, after skimming for a few minutes, go back and read for important details that were also mentioned in class. Practice beginning each assignment in this way, systematically and with a purpose in mind, and you will develop your study skills so that you make more efficient use of your time. You will more readily understand complex theories and complicated directions. Skim first, and then go back and read for details.

Vocabulary Skills

Vocabulary skills are also an integral part of developing your study strategy. In Chapter V we shall learn how to recognize key parts of words and understand them in various contexts, and also how to expand your expressive vocabulary as you explore new concepts in word meanings. What is important at this stage is to begin using the dictionary more and more, daily if possible. Look up two new words each day and use them in conversation or in your writing. Be especially alert to those you hear in class or at your work. Discover their proper usage as well as their etymology or origin.

Where to Find Information

Sometimes, no matter how hard you try to find the right answer, you cannot seem to locate it. Or you may not have enough information to complete your assigned task. Well, remember, there are a lot of resources all around you. It's just a matter of knowing where to look. Many students make a practice of studying in the library where encyclopedias and dictionaries are always available. In fact, your library contains records, tape recordings, programmed learning kits, and other self-teaching materials that cover a wide range of topics. You will also find a variety of periodicals (magazines and newspapers) that will give you access to a world of current events and put them into historical perspective as well. Learn to use these along with other learning aids such as filmstrips, educational video tapes, and of course, computer programs. Explore what each can do to help you get through your difficult assignments. Learn about these resources and how they can be utilized to lessen your frustrations and enhance your study skills and your efforts to attain your educational and personal goals.

A Learning Survey

Our study sessions can be an exciting adventure, a quest into the unknown, if we know exactly what we need to know and why. But, first we need to decide how much time and energy we must expend, and then we can plan a systematic course of action. So, let's take a short break here and turn our attention to what it is we enjoy learning. What is boring to us? What is trivial? What is interesting? Stimulating?

Curiosity and self-motivation can take us a long way on our journey. Our path of learning calls for difficult uphill climbing and pleasurable downhill jogging. Stop for a moment. Think about the last time you really enjoyed what you were learning. To help you get started, complete MY LEARNING SURVEY.

MY LEARNING SURVEY

My hobbies are	My pet peeves are
1)_____	_____
2)_____	_____

Easy to learn	Difficult to learn
1)_____	_____
2)_____	_____

Find out about your study strengths and weaknesses by checking below:

	Yes	No
A) Do I have a strategy for learning something each day?	_____	_____
B) If so, do I practice using this strategy regularly?	_____	_____
C) Do I set learning limits for myself? (time, effort)	_____	_____
D) Do I find learning a rewarding experience?	_____	_____
E) Do I have difficulty getting started on my assignments?	_____	_____
F) Do I skim to familiarize myself with assigned work?	_____	_____
G) Do I always understand the directions?	_____	_____
H) Do I know how to get help when I need it?	_____	_____
I) Do I have difficulty discussing my work with others?	_____	_____
J) Do my reading/writing abilities slow me down?	_____	_____
K) Do I know how to find the meanings of new words?	_____	_____
L) Am I a good speller?	_____	_____
M) Do I give up too easily when I become frustrated?	_____	_____
N) Do my future plans include using better study habits?	_____	_____

Study Strategies for Initial Learning Improvement

Did the learning survey indicate areas that need further improvement? Then, begin by using these study strategies on your next assignment.

Study Strategy #1
Read All Directions and Plan Ahead

Check your class notes and read all assignment directions. Make sure that you have enough time, supplies, and learning resources to complete the task.

Do I understand all directions?   Yes_____ No_____
What is the first thing I need to do to begin?_____
What books and learning resources are required?_____
How long should this assignment take me?   Hrs._____ mins._____
This assignment will be completed only after_____

My next assignment:_____
Do I understand all directions?   Yes_____ No_____
What is the first thing I need to do to begin?_____
What books and learning resources are required?_____
How long should this assignment take me?   Hrs. _____ mins. _____
This assignment will be completed only after_____

Study Strategy #2
Organize Your Study Time Wisely

Check the clock to determine how much time you will need to complete your assignments. Decide exactly how much time you will spend (1) skimming, (2) reading, and (3) answering questions. BUT DON'T BEGIN UNTIL YOU UNDERSTAND ALL DIRECTIONS. Now, give yourself an extra ten minutes to complete all work. In this way, you will soon become aware of your own true "learning limits": your attention span, fatigue time, and saturation (or brain drain) point.

I study best between the hours of _____ and _____.
It will take me approximately _____mins. to skim this assignment.
It will take me approximately _____mins. to read this assignment.
It will take me approximately _____mins. to complete my work.

If you get behind in your assignments due to illness, plan to make up all missed work at a time convenient to both you and your teacher. Otherwise, keep up with assignments as they are given to you. Put aside other nonrelated activities until after they are completed. Review those assignments often and you will remember more information that will be needed for future tests. Also, take the time to review your assignments to see if you missed any part. Pick up your own mistakes and incomplete work before your teacher sees it. This, too, will help you improve your chances for better grades.

Set aside a certain time each day for your study sessions. Use that time wisely by planning a study schedule when there will be a minimal amount of distraction. Then use the STUDY WARM-UPS in this book to help you get started on your work. By organizing your time, you are taking full responsibility for improving your study strategy, and you are taking control of your learning tasks.

Study Strategy #3
Investigate with Care

Be particular about what is stored in your brain. As you skim, familiarize yourself with what you are to learn, ask yourself questions, become curious about the facts you are assigned to learn, and begin fitting ideas together so that they make more sense. Connect those key words in the chapter with the chapter title and the subtopics. Stop and mentally summarize what you have read. Don't let any details get past you that you think will be important later on. Check it all out! Once you have found the main ideas in your reading, your oral and written responses for class assignments will be right on target.

Page Refresher

Use one of your reading assignments to practice looking for important details. First, skim through the chapter and then complete the following:

Pages to read in this assignment include ____ to ____
Important to go back and read more carefully__ __ __ __
Pages that may give me trouble__ __ __ __
Pages that I can skim quickly__ __ __ __
Pages that I know have answers on them __ __ __ __
Pages that are of interest to me__ __ __ __

Now, take a few minutes to study those easy pages first. But don't spend too much time on them. Next, go back and read the material that you think will give you some trouble. Remember, divide and— you guessed it! Attack all of your assignments in this systematic manner and your study sessions will be more enjoyable, make more sense, and go by a lot faster. Your time will be spent much more profitably, and your learning experiences will be much more meaningful.

Study Strategy #4
Be Versatile

There is a variety of ways to get your assignments under control. For example, learn to use those library resources we discussed earlier. Also, learn to study in small groups and brainstorm ideas that will help you get through major research projects. Look for supplemental reading on assigned topics at your local bookstore, as well as your school library. Be versatile in gaining new knowledge by experimenting. Learn what works best for you. Your time and money will be wisely spent if you discover how to decrease frustrations and increase your ability to learn and get better grades AND ENJOY DOING IT. Your versatility depends on what resources you have at your command.

MY RESOURCE LIST

Here is a list of names and telephone numbers of people I can call on to help me when I am studying:

Name_____   Phone #_____
Name_____   Phone #_____
Name_____   Phone #_____
Name_____   Phone #_____
Name_____   Phone #_____
Name_____   Phone #_____

Here is a list of books and other sources which will help me (you already have a dictionary, of course!):

Source_____   Subject_____
Source_____   Subject_____
Source_____   Subject_____
Source_____   Subject_____

You may also want to include a list of places where you can go for additional information:

1. _____ Hours Available _____ To _____
2. _____ Hours Available _____ To _____
3. _____ Hours Available _____ To _____

Use these resources to be versatile and aggressive as you work through your assignments. And don't be afraid to 'hound' your school librarian, teachers, school counselors, and anyone else who you think may be of some help to you. Knowing where to find needed information is only half the challenge of most learning tasks. Being a smart investigator, putting clues together, and discovering how each fact fits into the general scheme of things is, of course, the other half.

Now, let's take another short break. Go back and review what you have learned so far. Use your new study skills with all of your assignments. You will know that you are learning more effectively when you suddenly realize that you are getting more of your assignments completed, correctly, in less time. You will also begin feeling better about yourself, and your confidence and self-satisfaction will increase with each new learning experience. Use and modify your study skills for each of the subjects you must learn. Be systematic in this way and you will continue to improve your abilities to study more efficiently as you sidestep those frustrating moments that arise unexpectedly.

Don't read any further until you feel comfortable with this new study strategy. Make every effort to incorporate it into your daily study routine.

Study Warm-Ups

1. Rewrite the story of "Little Red Riding Hood" or one of your favorite fairy tales.
2. Rewrite the story in a freewheeling, humorous way by changing the characters, plot, and setting.
3. Now, ask someone to read your version and to draw a sketch of one of the characters.
4. With this STUDY WARM-UP, you can rewrite any stories in a class assignment. Be creative and use your imagination.

If you find this too easy, take a chapter read in your last class, or even a story you have seen on television. Rewrite it, adding your own unique twist to the plot. Make sketches at the end that will remind you about it later. Take the first few minutes of your study sessions to do this one. It will help you get in the mood for other writing assignments.

My Most Embarrassing Moments

Here is one of those rare STUDY WARM-UPS you may not want to share with others.

1. Write down the last three times you were really embarrassed:
   A) _____
   B) _____
   C) _____
2. Choose the one situation that you feel you can describe in detail most accurately (and without a lot of blushing!).

3. On a full sheet of paper, write down the incident leading up to the embarrassing situation, the embarrassing moment, and what happened afterward.

4. Add any feelings and thoughts you had or now have as you write.

Hey! You may know some embarrassing moments in other people's lives. Why not write about them as if you were writing a news article for your local newspaper (of course, actually publishing them or using them for blackmail is discouraged!).

Teachers, administrators, and their students know the value of silence within the walls of a classroom. With thirty or more children having thirty or more things to say all at once, concentration is all but impossible to maintain. And perhaps that is why most teachers encourage a quiet atmosphere throughout the school day.

Find a Quiet Place to Study

Most research suggests that you find a quiet place to study, a room with plenty of light and a minimum amount of noise. It takes a good deal of your energy to study a subject. When you tune in a radio station or turn on a television, your energy is being drawn from you that much faster; thus you are diminishing your ability to concentrate on the important details and concepts in your homework assignment. Learn to conserve your energy, concentrate on one thing at a time. Be relaxed, but also be mentally alert. When you do become tense or frustrated, stop and rest. Don't engage in a demanding activity during your rest period; you will probably not be refreshed enough to benefit by continued studying. So, rest your mind as well as your body. The time you actually spend on studying is based primarily on the following four conditions:

1. Your inner strength for maintaining interest and concentration.
2. Your ability to incorporate a working study strategy for learning.
3. The environment you are in while you study.
4. Your physical stamina (how quickly you become fatigued).

So, whenever possible, be well rested, and study in a quiet room, or a library that enforces some degree of quietness. Did you know that the value of libraries lies as much in their intellectual atmosphere as in their books? You will often be able to accomplish your study goals more easily in your school or local library and give your ego a boost at the same time. You will be surrounded by readily available learning materials on which you can depend for help. You will find that you are completing more of your assignments simply because you took the time to find a quiet place to work. The value of libraries and their study aids are discussed more fully in Chapter VII.

In summary, if you have difficulty settling down and concentrating on your assignments, go back to Chapter I and reread the section

"Ready-Steady-Study!" It is very important not only that you feel good about yourself, your study goals, and your past accomplishments, but also that you feel comfortable with your surroundings as you work through those assignments. You need to be in that place, at that time, for the express purpose of achieving your study goals. People find some strange but quiet places to get their work done: in closets, steam rooms, in the park under a tree, in an automobile, and, yes, even in a quiet corner of their local library.

WHERE I CONCENTRATE BEST

List three places where you can study and concentrate best:

1. _____
2. _____
3. _____

Encountering Problems

It is easy, sometimes, to let our personal problems get in our way. And when we lose our ability to learn, we also lose our capacity to concentrate and to cope with the assignments given us.

Health problems may be unavoidable. They have a way of distracting us from our intellectual pursuits. In this instance, however, priority must be given to rehabilitation of the body and mind first. Real and imagined health problems must be resolved before any meaningful learning can take place. Other problems you may encounter might be related to finances and social acceptance by peer groups. These problems can be handled more easily by consciously coming to grips with them. If you have tried and are unable to do this, you may want to consult a school counselor or psychologist among the many trained professionals on staff at various facilities both in education and in your community. Your learning experiences simply won't be satisfying if you are unable to meet your study goals.

Finally, vocational concerns will eventually present themselves, and if you are not prepared; they could be a real problem. Prepare yourself by exploring job-related subjects, finding out what aptitudes you have and what skills you will need. Not everyone knows what kind of a career he wants to enter even after graduating from college.

And this lack of a vocational goal may be a setback for you unless you experiment with a few academic majors in college or investigate various job-training programs provided by small businesses and large corporations. Before you decide on a career (1) find out the nature of that career, (2) discover what skills are required, (3) know what your chances are for promotion, higher salary, working conditions, and (4) try to determine the needs for employees in this field in the near future.

Learn for a Better Future

At this point, let's make some commitments to ourselves to ensure a bright and prosperous future. First, let's make a commitment to meet whatever hardships and disillusionment come our way with resolved determination to cope with them as intelligently as we know how. Second, let's make a commitment to learn, to practice, and to live by those ideas and ideals that will make our lives and the lives of those around us happier. Finally, learn the value of having a positive self-esteem, and further, plan for a more successful future by having personal goals that you know you can achieve. Make your learning goals a reality with persistence and practice.

The key to adhering to those commitments is to learn all you want to know when you want to know. Begin today: look all around you—OBSERVE, OBSERVE, OBSERVE. Look for the unusual, the unique. Anticipate the new, but don't overlook those old details that have survived as wisdom for centuries.

In summary, if we anticipate problems and plan to overcome them with determination, and then if we look to the future and anticipate its needs as well as our own, we can set realistic goals and, with dedication and commitment, we can find personal fulfillment. Further, we can look to the past in our efforts to meet our educational needs in the future. With tongue in cheek, Will Rogers, the famous homespun philosopher of the early 1930s, once remarked:

> "I believe the Lord split knowledge up among His subjects about equal. The so-called ignorant are happy. Maybe they're happy 'cause they know enough to be happy. The smart one, he knows he knows a lot, and that makes him unhappy 'cause

he can't impart it to all of his friends. I guess discontent is in proportion to knowledge. The more you know, the more you realize you don't know.''

And yet, is it not also true that in striving for truth we discover a real sense of ourselves and who we are in relation to our reality?

Study Warm-Ups

Meeting My Needs

Abraham Maslow's hierarchy of needs* are often viewed as motivating factors people consider essential when they want to persuade others. They also represent a focal point for self-motivation. Think about each of his five categories. Then (1) identify a specific need you have right now for each of them, (2) write down a plan to meet each of those needs, and (3) describe exactly how one or more of your needs can be met as you begin your next assignment.

Maslow's Hierarchy of Needs

Physiological needs: _____

Safety needs: _____

Love needs: _____

Esteem needs: _____

Self-actualization: _____

How can the next assignment meet my own needs? _____

---

*You will find an interesting discussion of Maslow's needs in his book *Toward a Psychology of Being*.

Your Career = Your Skills

Do you have the skills required for the career you want? Make a list of various kinds of jobs that require the following skills and abilities.

A) Use of special equipment (computer tools, heavy machines)

_____   _____

_____   _____

B) Explaining or speaking with some authority

_____   _____

_____   _____

C) Reading and writing technical material

_____   _____

_____   _____

D) Use of numerical equations and sound reasoning

_____   _____

_____   _____

Now, make a list of other skills and occupations that you have explored:

Job Skills   Occupations

_____   _____

_____   _____

_____   _____

_____   _____

Where can I get the knowledge and skills I need for the kind of job I want?

_____

_____

Self-Contract

Here is a self-contract to motivate you to do the job you set out to do. Note that this contract involves another person: the overseer, responsible for supporting your efforts, encouraging you to meet your goals, and giving you agreed-upon rewards.

My name:_____   Date: _____
Name of overseer: _____
My goal is to _____

My commitment:
I agree to   _____
_____

Overseer's Commitment:
I agree to   _____
_____

CONSEQUENCES AND REWARDS

If I keep my contract, I will _____
If I fail to keep my contract, I will _____
If contract is kept, overseer will reward me in the following manner:

A)_____
    B)_____
    C)_____

Date contract is to be completed:_____ Time: _____
My signature_____ Overseer's signature _____

CHAPTER IV

Making Sense Out of Assignments

THOUGHT: I am not ashamed to confess that I am ignorant of what I do not know.

Cicero

Many students, especially at the secondary school level, find it difficult to go from one class to another, remembering the page numbers, directions, and due dates for their assignments. The key lies in never walking out of a classroom with only a vague notion of what has been assigned. The study strategy here is an easy one — keep alert! You must develop your abilities to take notes, ask questions, and determine what you are being asked to do. Make the effort so many students shy away from; ask questions when you are unsure of how to proceed or when you become confused as assignments are given. Remember, your teachers are paid to explain and to re-explain procedures and methodologies. Once you feel you understand not only the directions but also the purpose of the assignment, you will have bypassed several major hurdles in doing your class- and homework assignments, and you will find your learning tasks more challenging and more rewarding.

Skim and Scan

Here is another STUDY STRATEGY to help you get started. Skim and scan all material you are assigned before you get down to work. Find out where you are most likely to find the important details and potential answers before you 'dive in.' Have paper and pencil at your desk to jot down the page numbers of key words, main ideas, and major sections in the chapters that will need closer inspection later on in your study session; this will be a great time-saver for you, and your written notes will help you refer back to important pages more quickly. After you have taken approximately three to five minutes skimming and scanning your material, go back and read a little more carefully for details that you think are vital. Periodically, stop your reading. Sit back, relax, and ask yourself, ''Is what I just read or figured out meaningful? How?'' Think about what you are learning; put the directions, concepts, and main ideas into perspective. The more relevant you can make your assignment, the more interesting it will become, and the more interesting, the longer you will tend to remember what you learned. Memorize formulas, rules, principles, and concepts that will be essential for you to know later on tests and other assignments. Challenge yourself to discover what the author is trying to say. In this way, you will be actively involved, unlocking doors to new knowledge, and gaining insight into information that now makes more sense.

Note-Taking

One of the most important times to pay close attention in a class is in when your teacher is explaining an assignment. Take careful notes when assignments are being discussed. Write clearly enough so that you can read and understand your notes when it is time to refer back to them. As you listen for important information to write down, be sure you (1) understand and accurately record the assignment and all of the examples, (2) copy the directions as given, a step at a time, (3) know the date your assignment is to be completed and turned in to your teacher, and (4) understand how all your previous work will help you do this assignment. Also, try to find out exactly how the assignment will be evaluated or graded. Make it a practice to take no fewer than a half page of notes per assignment; more is better! Later, you will want to rewrite and review your notes. So, keep them orderly and separate them from other notes in other classes. If you have done a good job of note-taking, many of the questions that come to mind as you begin the assignment will be answered because you took the time to listen and record those explanations and examples.

Math and Science Assignments

The questions and problems in these classes are usually assigned to give students practice in remembering and utilizing formulas, laws, and concepts. Some asssignments are designed to help you memorize terminology and other data. Other assignments are given to see if you can demonstrate some degree of competency in their application. Here are five study steps to follow as you work with these assignments:

Step 1: Examine the examples whenever possible.
Step 2: Follow all procedures step-by-step.
Step 3: Double check the directions; they are your 'blueprint.'
Step 4: If you become confused, ask someone a question— get help!
Step 5: Above all, don't let yourself be frustrated. Grit your teeth and start again.

Discover a different angle when studying a complicated concept or formula. Find out where you can get another perspective or added information when you need it. There are many places to look for answers. Ask teachers, librarians, friends, and parents; contact instructors at learning centers at colleges and churches. Yes, it takes a little time and a little courage to seek out the right person to ask the right question at the right time—but in the long run, it will save you a lot of grief. Anyway, most people feel good when asked for advice, and they admire your willingness to look for the answers. And if they do not have the answer you need, they may know where you can find it.

History and Social Studies Assignments

The work assigned in these classes requires that you learn about important people, places, dates, and events. For these assignments, be sure to skim and scan before you read slowly through material. This way you will be alerted to where those names, dates, and events appear and you will be able to associate them with other ideas in the chapter. Then, when you are ready to work on the assigned material, read the directions carefully to determine exactly how you are to respond using those names, dates, and events. Julie Kessleman-Turkel and Franklynn Peterson have compiled a list of terms that usually point out to students what specific response is called for in various kinds of assignments.

Name, list, tell, and *enumerate* all mean to give just the information that is specifically asked for.

Summarize and *outline* mean to give the main points.

Define means to give the meaning.

Justify means to give the facts that prove it is true.

Prove means to show that it is true and that its opposite is false.

Discuss and *review* mean to examine from all angles.

Compare means to show how things are the same and how they differ.

Contrast means to give your opinion as to advantages and disadvantages.

Criticize means to examine the pros and cons and give your judgment.

Explain means to show, in logical sequence, how or why something happened.

These are important key words to be aware of as you interpret assigned problems or questions for these and similar courses. Read the directions carefully and do not begin work until you have a clear idea of what is expected. For example, knowing what dates or events you are to write about for what purpose will guide your responses as you complete the assignment.

The Importance of Understanding Questions

The essence of any effective study strategy lies in your ability to examine questions that you are asked. If the primary function of a teaching unit is to focus your attention on factual knowledge, certain types of questions will tend to be asked. If your teachers are interested in how you organize or analyze certain kinds of knowledge, questions of a different nature will be assigned. Moreover, some teachers deal with teaching the kinds of concepts which include creative thought, queries and subjectivity in nature, and of course, there are questions designed just for this purpose.

Recall Questions

When you are expected to learn certain specific facts such as dates, names of famous people, geographical locations, or factual information that must be studied beforehand, you are learning primarily for the purpose of recalling information for tests and quizzes. So, when your science teacher asks you a question such as ''What bone is connected to the leg bone, thigh bone, etc.'' you are expected to respond with a specific answer. Your response will indicate whether or not you have a firm grasp of the fundamental terms or ideas necessary to progress to more advanced learning experiences. These kinds of questions are often referred to as questions of fact. If your teacher wants more from you than simply extracting factual knowledge from your head, he will have to ask a question of a different nature.

Descriptive Questions

You can identify these kinds of questions by the way they are asked: (1) Describe the characteristics, (2) In what way does A affect B? (3) Compare this with that, and (4) What were the main differences between set X and set Y? Your teachers now assume that you already know the facts. You are asked to distinguish, describe, compare, and contrast those facts. So, you must first recall the facts and then fill in your response with appropriate data in some clear and organized fashion.

Explanatory Questions

This kind of question challenges your ability to analyze a statement. You are expected to give some sound reasoning for picking an answer, or to show a clear cause-effect relationship. You are required not only to pick the right answer, but also to justify or give good reasons why you chose it. Unlike the recall question, you must come up with more than just the right response. ''Why did the chemical react in this fashion under these circumstances?'' and ''What might have been a possible solution to this battle between the States?'' are examples of this kind of question.

Synthesizing Questions

''Based upon what you have just heard in this discussion, what are your conclusions?'' and ''What are four implications of this author?'' are examples of questions a teacher would ask to see how you might combine certain ideas or bits of information to substantiate your response. Your major task here is to state a relationship among previously unrelated ideas. This type of question may also be referred to as a question of policy.

Judgmental Questions

These questions offer you a chance to respond using a set of criteria, alternatives, or characteristics that may have certain advantages and disadvantages. Your task is to make a 'judgment call.' Here, you are expected to choose the best answer and substantiate your choice. "Which important factors contribute to high unemployment? Why?'' and "Which of the following solutions do you think will solve this problem more economically?'' are examples of this kind of questioning. These questions necessitate some standard by which you must make your evaluation. Such standards or criteria are usually spelled out in one of your class discussions. Check your notes rather carefully when studying for this one. This kind of question is also referred to as a question of value.

Open-Ended Questions

These may be essay type questions you are to answer. Often, you must not only depend on your reading, your notes, and your memory of class discussion, but you are required to use a little imagination too. The value of such questions is to encourage you to search for hidden meanings, unanalyzed relationships, or speculation on the unknown. Your answer will often be open to debate because there may not be 'one correct answer' to the question. For instance, you may be asked a question similar to these: "What will be the predominant mode of transportation in the year 2000?'' or "If you were given the ability to create life, what human characteristics would you classify as the most important? Why?''

Understand the Question Before You Answer

If you are given an assignment in which questions like these are asked, know how to interpret and study them. You have heard the expression 'fight fire with fire.' Well, that is just what you must do. Ask questions about questions you do not understand. Check each step you are to follow to see if they all make sense. Then answer the questions as specifically and as accurately as you can. When you have finished the assignment (1) proofread for careless mistakes, (2) go back over the directions, the questions, and your answers to see whether you have left anything out, and (3) keep in mind the overall purpose of the assignment. Remember, find out what kind of answers your teacher wants for the type of questions he asks.

Problem-Solving

Many class projects, including research, experiments, computer-related activities and examinations, are designed to help you develop your thinking abilities. One problem-solving strategy is readily available for you when those assignments become too complicated to handle. Here is the problem-solving strategy in a nutshell:

1. Define the nature of your problem (or topic)—find out the importance of the problem. Whom does it affect? How did it become a major concern?
2. Analyze the problem from all angles—Again, divide and conquer. Understand the different aspects of the problem. Why has it become significant? What factors contribute to the problem?
3. Search for possible solutions—Find out how others have solved this kind of problem. Which solutions worked the best? Why? Are any of these alternatives workable under the present circumstances?
4. Choose the best solution—find the best solution that is feasible. Who will be affected? What will be the cost?
5. Implement your solution—show how you can get your plan off the drawing board and into practice. What should be done first? second? third, etc.

Problems such as "How can we clean up the environment?" and "What program should replace the Social Security System?" are typical classroom-assigned problems for which you are expected to research facts, justify decisions, and produce a workable policy or program that is superior to the one already in place.

When your English or Social Studies teacher gives you a similar topic, begin your problem-solving by gathering information to build a case for your particular solution or point of view. Your solution will be accepted or rejected based upon how thoroughly you researched the topic. Being unbiased and objective is the key to this approach. Close scrutiny of every possible aspect of the problem under investigation is encouraged. Evidence and sound reasoning are evaluated here. You can utilize this problem-solving approach for many other writing assignments, as we will discuss later.

Public Speaking

When your assignment is to present a speech, give an oral book report, or participate in a group discussion, you need to begin by knowing (1) what you want to say, and (2) how you want to say it. Gather information on the assigned topic; use note cards to organize this data into a logical sequence. Then decide what your main purpose will be: to inform, to persuade, or to entertain your audience.

Practice Your Oral Presentation Several Times

Using your notes, rehearse your oral presentation in a conversational manner. Do not simply read and memorize them. Practice presenting your ideas logically, expressing them in different words, as you would do while explaining something to someone in a normal conversation. The more familiar you become with ways of expressing your ideas, the more comfortable you will be when you actually present your speech to an audience. The more you practice, the less stage fright you will experience.

Use words that your audience will understand. Include interesting statistics and examples of your main thoughts. You may also find visual aids very helpful if you are not accustomed to presenting speeches. Utilize charts and graphs to show your audience what you are talking about. Use them as an outline and reminder of your speech as it develops.

Another prerequisite for presenting an effective speech is your desire to communicate your ideas. If you feel you have some interesting thoughts to share with your audience, they, in turn, will feel it worthwhile to listen to what you have to say. So, speak with enthusiasm and learn to enjoy presenting speeches. Remember those two major criteria for giving an effective speech:

Know what to say—Here you are demonstrating your ability to express your ideas clearly, logically, and interestingly. Use transitions between your major points. Help your audience follow your train of thought by organizing your ideas in a chronological, cause-effect, spatial, or other logical pattern.

And how to say it—Here your nonverbal communication (posture, gestures, and facial expressions) is evaluated. Maintain eye contact with your audience; stand relaxed and use gestures as you normally would in everyday conversation. Chewing gum, playing with your hair, or tapping your fingers on the podium are distracting features you will want to curb for this particular assignment.

Writing Assignments

Language Arts assignments evolve from class readings or themes that are assigned by the teacher or agreed upon by consensus of the class. When you begin work on these writing exercises find out (1) the exact wording of the theme, (2) the length and the specific format required for this exercise, (3) date the assignment is due, (4) whether you are required to include a rough draft, footnotes, bibliography, etc., and (5) the criteria by which your teacher will judge your writing (spelling, grammar, organization). Once you understand these requirements, you can more easily plan your study goals.

The Challenge: Control Your Writing

Here are five suggestions that will help you the next time you are asked to compose prose:

• Identify something familiar about the theme assigned.
• Limit the theme to something you can write about from your knowledge or past experience.
• Jot down ideas first. Then organize them in some logical fashion.
• Use language that will express your ideas clearly AND will get the best evaluation from your teacher.
• Write simply, clearly, and concisely—always!

In summary, meet the requirements for each written and oral assignment you are given and strive for excellence in your self-expression. Give yourself the advantage of a quiet, comfortable room in which to work. Stick with each task until you have completed it. Use your time wisely! Be sure you have plenty of time to meet the deadline. Promise yourself to complete your next assignment by:

Time limit: Hrs.__Mins.__Sec.__(plus 10 minutes)

Study Warm-Up

Assignment Journal

Here is your chance to tell those assignments exactly what you think of them. Keep all dates, directions, and personal comments in your journal for the next month and don't be afraid to include your personal observations or 'blow off a little steam' while writing.

1. Write down what you were feeling while working on the assignment.
2. Always include the date for reference.
3. Make a half-page entry (or more) each day.
4. Set aside twenty minutes to write down your impressions each day (you will be surprised how much better you will feel afterward!).

5. If you cannot think of anything to write, try answering these
    questions:

    A)How am I improving my study strategy?
    B)What weaknesses must I overcome?
    C)What am I feeling right now? Why?
    D)What changes need to be made in my study schedule?
    E) What kinds of assignments frustrate me the most? Why?
    F) Why should I do this assignment?
    G)How will I feel after I have finished the next assignment?

Taking Your Assignment to Task

What subject is being studied right now? _____

What is the main concept or example I need to know? _____

What else do I need to know about this assignment? _____

How do I feel about this assignment? _____

In order to get started, what must I do first? _____

How can I make this assignment more meaningful? _____

How long should this assignment take me? _____

How will I know when I am finished? _____

Extra notes that will help me work through the assignment: _____

_____
_____
_____
_____
_____
_____
_____

Assignment Details

What is the assignment? _____

What is the purpose of this assignment? _____

_____

In which class was this assignment given? _____

What books/materials do I need? _____

These are the exact instructions for the assignment: _____

_____

_____

_____

Special instructions:

_____

_____

How will this assignment be graded? _____

_____

Study aids/people I can depend on when I have a question: _____

_____

What do I think my grade will be on this assignment? _____

What grade would I give myself for my efforts? _____

Questions I have about this assignment: _____

_____

_____

_____

CHAPTER V

Improve Your Vocabulary

THOUGHT: The difference between the right word and the almost right word is the difference between lightning and the lightning bug.

Mark Twain

Improving your vocabulary is a major part of any study strategy improvement program. You already know thousands of words. The more words you understand, of course, the more meaning you will derive from subjects you study. No matter what your status is in life, no matter what your age, your social or economic background, you can gain more knowledge through a better acquaintance with spoken and written symbols, words. Just by taking a few minutes a day, you can improve your vocabulary. So, concentrate and practice conscientiously as you strive for a better command of the language.

You really have two vocabularies that are interrelated. The first is your *receptive* vocabulary. As we mentioned before, you have the ability to read and listen with good comprehension because you have learned some 60,000 words already. Although you may not be able to define all of them, you have a good working knowledge of what each of them means.

The total number of words you use from your *expressive* vocabulary is much less. We actively communicate with others by using fewer than 1,000 words. But with a little determination and perseverance, we can add to this vocabulary by becoming aware of new words and using them to express our ideas more fully, more meaningfully. All you need to do is set your mind to the task of learning more words on a daily basis. You can find new words in newspaper and magazine articles, as well as those introduced to you at school and on the job.

Introduce Yourself to New Words

At this point, you may be saying to yourself, ''I am not a good speller, never learned the right meanings of words and probably never will.'' Well, let's start by developing a more positive attitude. If you want to be a better speller, you can be. If you want to be a whiz at crossword puzzles by knowing the meanings of more words, you can do that too. And here is the key: become familiar with the three essential elements of any word: (1) how the word looks, or how the word is spelled correctly, (2) what the word means, or how it is used in different situations, and (3) the etymology or historical origin of the word. You will find words a lot easier to remember if you concentrate on these three elements as you meet them.

The derivation helps you remember parts of words. Learn the meanings of the beginning letters called *prefixes*, the *root* letters, and the common endings known as *suffixes*. By learning the historical origin of a word, you learn to identify other words that are spelled similarly. For example, when you study the word *crucial*, you quickly discover that it is derived from the Latin word for cross. Knowing that, you can make some interesting connections to other words that are similar in spelling. You will readily recognize common meanings in such words as *crucify, crusade,* and *crux*.

Learn the common meanings of prefixes, suffixes, and roots as you study words in English class. They will be an invaluable way to unlock new words you come across in other courses. Also, make a habit of remembering a word that has the same meaning as the one you are studying. Such words are called *synonyms*. These are often easier to remember than the full definition. You may also want to know words that are opposite in meaning; these words are referred to as *antonyms*.

Put each new word you learn in a Vocabulary Notebook. Keep an up-to-date file of the way these words might be used throughout your day. Put them in categorical lists labeled ''Must Know Words for School,'' ''Must Know Words for My Hobby,'' etc. Don't forget to investigate those on-the-job expressions often referred to as 'shop-talk.' Notice how these words are used in context. Do they have a different meaning in more popular settings? How?

Word Usage

Be more conscious of the way people express their own ideas. Listen critically and find out the meanings of those words you hear all around you. Perceive those words in their own special context, in the light of the situation, by the subject being discussed, or by the communicator's particular use of words. This may sound easier than it really is. Take the word *run*, for example. Is the speaker referring to someone who *runs* to the train station? A child who *runs* a high temperature while sick in bed? Or perhaps he was talking about the play the quarterback had just *run* in the football game. Perhaps he was describing the *run* he noticed in a young woman's nylon stocking, or the *run* he saw in a baseball game last night. Let's see, have we *run* through all the meanings yet?

How do some words get so many definitions? Well, lexicographers or writers of dictionaries gather examples of words people use to symbolize what they are trying to convey to someone else. These examples are written in the form of definitions to describe those many meanings. That is why such a word as *strike* can be meaningful when we talk about baseball, bowling, fishing, a labor-management dispute, or someone who has been prospecting for gold.

Accurate Words

Words should not be regarded as right or wrong words. They are words that are used accurately or inaccurately when people try to symbolize their feelings and ideas. If a word is to say exactly what you want it to say, you must first understand that word's denotative and connotative meanings in the first place. Remember, words mean different things to different people.

Denotation and Connotation

In order to express our ideas intelligently (and, after all, isn't that our primary goal?) we need to know their dictionary definition and also the overtone or implied meaning, and which is which. For instance, in your Science class, your teacher may be looking for a specific meaning when he asks you to define photosynthesis. Likewise, your Math teacher will probably be looking for a specific response to the question, ''What is Pythagorean theory?'' In short, the denotation of a word is simply the core meaning, which can be corroborated by using a glossary, a dictionary, or another reference such as a thesaurus or an encyclopedia.

The connotative meanings of a word, on the other hand, are not quite so clear-cut and exact. Many words are often shaded by certain positive or negative associations that deviate from the more specific meaning. Take the word *fox*, for example. This word may be used to denote a four-legged animal with a bushy tail, or it may be used in a connotative way to refer to a two-legged animal with, well, you get the picture. This more figurative usage may contain emotional overtones, whereas a strictly denotative one would not. Here is another way to distinguish these kinds of meaning: Denotative uses of words are often associated with exact sciences, and connotative uses of words are found in poetic and figuratively written literature.

Beware of Overused Words

It is sometimes "cool" to use slang words. But they tend to become overused and obsolete quickly. Such overused words are also called clichés—trite, hackneyed, and shopworn expressions that have very little meaning. Words such as *dude, chic,* and *totally awesome* hinder your ability to say what you really mean. They block out our true thoughts and feelings. So, learn to replace overused words with more concise ones. Don't be misled into thinking that these words are always "cool to say." Instead, develop your own personal Word File to give your thoughts and feelings more word power.

MY WORD FILE

Learn the meaning of these words by noting their denotative and connotative meanings:

Denotation	Word	Connotation
_____	Limousine	_____
_____	Buggy	_____
_____	Chicken	_____
_____	Witch	_____
_____	Dump	_____
_____	Cross	_____

	Hurdle	
_____	Crowd	_____
_____	Gruesome	_____
_____	Gross	_____

Now that you have the idea, write down ten new words of your own that you can use to replace those old, worn-out ones:

_____ _____ _____
_____ _____ _____
_____ _____ _____
_____ _____ _____
_____ _____ _____
_____ _____ _____
_____ _____ _____
_____ _____ _____
_____ _____ _____
_____ _____ _____

Appropriate Words

Watch out for words that easily confuse people. There are a few that may be misconstrued due to regional dialects and usages. For example, one person from the West might be well acquainted with a couch on his front porch. But someone from the South may be more comfortable with a divan on his stoop. There are also levels of language to consider. "I have learned my lessons quite well" and "Dat's a lot o'stuff I got to learn, I can tell ya," are examples of extreme language levels. The connotation of the second utterance invites a listener to assume that the speaker is not well educated. So, here we can see a glaring difference between the first sentence, which is in Standard English, and the second, which would be labeled Nonstandard English. Again, neither level of language is right or wrong; both simply exist appropriately or inappropriately in a given communication situation.

Etymology

It is common for words to change not only in meaning, but also in spelling and pronunciation. Most words in any language have a history, and it is interesting to study how they came about, when, and where, and what changes they have gone through to get to their present form. This is known as the etymology of words. As you study new words in this way, you will find some fascinating events surrounding their usage. In fact, many books discussing the origins of words can be found in your library or bookstore.

Don't forget to check in your work manual and other job-related publications for those 'shoptalk' terms called jargon. These particular words have grown out of necessity to be concise, meaningful, and specific. You will be further ahead if you have a working knowledge of these terms as you enter your chosen occupation.

Root Words

An important clue to the meanings of a word is the root of the word. This is the combination of letters that holds the core meaning. Once you have learned the meaning of one root word, many other words are automatically learned as well. Here is an example:

Root word: Form
Related words: Formation, information, reformation

In this example, the root word is form, which refers to shape or structure of something. The other words have related meanings, which are easy to learn if you know about their prefixes and suffixes. Now, you try one. Using *judge* as the root word, see if you can find three related words:

Root word: judge
Related words: _____   _____   _____

Now that you have the idea, try a couple on your own:

Root word: _____
Related words: _____   _____   _____
Root Word: _____
Related words: _____   _____   _____

Using the Dictionary

Good dictionaries are compiled from a variety of sources such as textbooks, library books, popular magazines, and technical journals. They are intended to help you familiarize yourself with new words as you come across them, whether you are reading business journals, newspapers, children's literature, or modern or classical novels and books.

For convenience, words are entered in alphabetical order. If two words begin with the same letter, they are alphabetized according to the second letter, then the third and fourth, and so on.

Guide Words

To further help you locate a word, lexicographers place a guide word, usually printed in boldface type, in the top corner of each page. The guide words indicate the first and last words entered on that particular page. So, be sure to look there first, using your skimming and scanning skills to find the definitions you are after.

The A-B-C's of Dictionaries

Alphabetize these words. Then find a word in a dictionary and write the two guide words at the top of the page.

| invade | anthem | broker | present | preparatory |
| retain | impose | faithful | recognize | speculate |

Words   *Guide Words*

1._____   _____ _____
2._____   _____ _____
3._____   _____ _____
4._____   _____ _____
5._____   _____ _____
6._____   _____ _____
7._____   _____ _____

8._____   _____ _____
9._____   _____ _____
10._____   _____ _____

As you work through this activity, note how your dictionary divides each word into syllables. Sometimes this can help you in learning the correct pronunciation. Also, note that each is identified as to the part of speech it is and whether it is singular or plural. These are usually indicated by abbreviations. Check the front of your dictionary for an explanation of the symbols used.

In summary, the dictionary is designed to describe how we use words, to inform us of various aspects of our language, and to give us a better sense of how to use words more appropriately. During your study sessions, use it often to look up new terms. Even though it does not have all the answers you may be looking for, it certainly has some valuable clues as to where you can gain more knowledge.

A Word May Have Many Meanings

The 500 most used words in the English language have at least 14,000 definitions. The fact that a number of meanings may be assigned to a given word explains why messages are subject to misinterpretation and why our communication is open to misunderstandings. With such odds against us, it becomes a real challenge to convey a specific meaning or intent successfully.

This poem,* for example, contains a number of words that are commonly used to represent a variety of objects:

Where can a man buy a cap for his knee?
Or a key for a lock of his hair?
Can your eyes be called an academy
Because there are pupils there?
In the crown of your head
What jewels are found?
Who crosses the bridge of your nose?
Could you use a shingle in the roof of your mouth?

*From *Understanding and Being Understood* by Dr. Sanford I. Berman, International Society for General Semantics, 1969, p. 13.

Nails in the end of your toes?
Could you sit in the shade of the palm of your hand?
Or beat on the drum of your ear?
Does the calf of your leg eat the corn on your toe?
Then why grow corn on the ear?

"*Must Words*" to Know

If you find yourself scratching your head in confusion while sitting in class as the teacher uses terms you never heard of, maybe it is time to double-check your understanding of some ''must words'' that are constantly used in particular fields of study. Use a dictionary to look up any of the following that you don't know. Be sure you understand the definitions of these words. Add other words that you have heard but did not know.

PHYSICAL EDUCATION

PHYSICAL FITNESS	FOOTBALL	SOCCER
exercise	down	dribble
agility	formation	goalkeeper
endurance	fumble	linesman
posture	interception	offside
unfit	lateral pass	penalty

BASKETBALL	BASEBALL	TRACK & FIELD
backboard	balk	field events
forward	bunt	lap
foul	inning	relay
guards	mound	baton
screen	sacrifice	meters

YOUR WORDS:
_____   _____   _____   _____
_____   _____   _____   _____

HEALTH

antiseptic	larynx	rabies
carbohydrate	nutrition	respiration
dehydrated	orthodontist	stimulant
exhalation	oxidation	vaccination
hemoglobin	penicillin	virus
immunize	pollution	
inhalation	protein	

HISTORY

communism	industry	prohibition
constitution	isolationism	republic
crisis	judiciary	revolution
currency	lame duck	statesman
democracy	leadership	tariff
filibuster	neutrality	treaty

YOUR WORDS:

_____ _____ _____ _____

_____ _____ _____ _____

_____ _____ _____ _____

_____ _____ _____ _____

ENGLISH

antonym	eight parts of speech	prefix
character	etymology	propaganda
climax	homonym	root
compound	linguistics	semantics
comprehension	metaphor	setting
connotation	narrative	simile
consonant	phonetics	suffix
denotation	plot	synonym
		vowel

SCIENCE

amphibian	behavior	geology
Aristotle	Bell, Alexander G.	glands
astronaut	biology	homo sapiens
atmosphere	conservation	photosynthesis
atom	dinosaur	theory
bacteria	electron	

YOUR WORDS:

_____ _____ _____ _____

_____ _____ _____ _____

_____ _____ _____ _____

_____ _____ _____ _____

MATHEMATICS

abscissa	integer	sine
axiom	logarithm	slope
cube	null	tangent
differential	obtuse	theorem
exponent	opposite	trinomial
factor	power	union
infinity	pi	variable

Study Warm-Ups

Digging Out the Roots

Find the root in each of the following words. Then write a word
that you know has the same root. Check your dictionary if necessary.

Word	Root	Your Example
1. rearrange		
2. bloodline		
3. cheapskate		
4. denounce		
5. equalize		
6. futuristic		
7. generic		
8. hemoglobin		
9. illegible		
10. judicial		
11. kinesis		
12. lawmaker		
13. memorandum		
14. negation		
15. orthopedic		
16. parenthesis		
17. quota		
18. ratify		
19. sanitary		
20. telecommunication		

Expanding Your Vocabulary

Find the etymology of each of the following words. Use an un-
abridged dictionary, encyclopedia, or other source to help you. Also
write down what you think are the most interesting facts about each.
Learn to use these words in your daily conversation:

rhetoric _____

informant _____

glib _____

articulate _____

etymology _____

deviation _____

subordinate _____

media _____

affiliate _____

composition _____

Find two of your own:

_____   _____

_____   _____

What similarities and differences have you noticed in these words?

Similarities: _____

_____

Differences: _____

_____

Word Power

1.   Learn to use the thesaurus as well as a standard dictionary.
2.   Always look up words related to your interests.
3.   In fact, why not begin this habit today? Learn a word a day.
4.   Try your hand at a crossword puzzle once a week.
5.   Make learning words a challenge. Write down new ones you hear.

Start by writing down five of your favorite words. Then use a thesaurus to find synonyms for them:

My Favorite Words   *Synonyms*

1) _____   _____

2) _____   _____

3) _____   _____

4) ———————————————   ———————————————
5) ———————————————   ———————————————

Now, find five new words that might help you express your ideas more clearly:

1) —————————————————————————————
2) —————————————————————————————
3) —————————————————————————————
4) —————————————————————————————
5) —————————————————————————————

After completing this STUDY WARM-UP, write down what you have discovered in general about word usage: ———————————

———————————————————————————————
———————————————————————————————
———————————————————————————————
———————————————————————————————
———————————————————————————————

CHAPTER VI

Reading Skills Are Vital

THOUGHT: Some books are to be tasted, others to be swallowed, and some few to be chewed and digested.

Jane Austen

Reading is a vital skill in your STUDY STRATEGY. Take time to read more newspapers, magazines, library books, and any other reading material you can get your hands on. But whatever you do, READ MORE! There is no real secret here in how to improve your reading skills. You must decide you want to redirect your energy, that's all. Rather than playing cards, watching television, or frequenting your local pub, sit down and discover the world of ideas. The more you read, the more you will improve your (1) vocabulary, (2) grades in school, (3) ability to understand more of what you read in less time, and (4) interest in new hobbies and new fields of academic endeavor. Start by stopping by your library, bookstore, or nearby learning center at least once a week and discovering what is available. Develop a positive attitude toward reading; trade in poor reading habits such as word-by-word reading and finger-pointing.

Are You a Poor Reader?

If the answer is maybe, or I'm really not sure, read on, and let's ask some questions that will help us discover how to become better readers. If you find that you have some of the following poor habits, perhaps it's time for you to make a concerted effort to change them.

Do You Read Without a Purpose?

Poor readers seldom know why they are reading an assigned chapter, a story, a play, or anything else. As a result, not much self-motivation or interest is generated. If they read at all, not much is comprehended, less is remembered afterward, and of course, frustration sets in and discourages them from reading further. Have you ever felt that reading something was a waste of time? Find a reason to read your assignments carefully, thoroughly, and don't let this poor reading habit slow you down, or discourage you from understanding the subjects you are studying.

Do You Read Word-by-Word?

The word-by-word reading skill you were taught in elementary school does not work well in secondary education. Poor readers remember very little of the beginning sentences after reading the last one in a paragraph. Result: poor comprehension. Surprisingly, you can learn more if you read faster. Your cognitive processes are able to connect many ideas and store them in your brain more accurately. So, if you think you are still using elementary reading skills on secondary reading assignments, stop! Thus, you will be able to increase your overall understanding of what you read.

Do You Have Only One Reading Rate?

Learn to scan and skim through your reading assignments of difficult material first. Then you will know how fast or how slowly you need to go to cover the material. You can read rapidly through stories and even novels to understand the author's main theme. But you may need to read more slowly through textbook chapters containing unfamiliar theories and concepts that you must learn in detail. So, pay close attention to the difficulty of the reading material, adjust your reading speed accordingly, and concentrate a little more. In this way you will be actively involved with your reading and your efforts will be rewarded.

Do You Believe Everything You Read?

Poor readers seldom ask questions about what they have read. Generally, they go along with whatever point of view the author presents. As a result, they are unable to see the forest for the trees! They fail to differentiate the important information from the interesting but perhaps trivial ideas. So always be critical and even skeptical as you read.

Do You Have a Limited Vocabulary?

Poor readers are usually not curious enough to stop reading and look up an unfamiliar word in the dictionary. On the contrary, they may not bother to finish reading the assignment when it gets too difficult. If the words are 'too hard' they simply give up in mid-passage. Understandably, this course of action is preferable to continuing in mounting frustration. Even when poor readers make an effort to trudge through their reading, or to look up new words at those moments they really need to know, they often have trouble because of their poorly developed reading skills. Such a waste of time and energy!

Do You Usually Read the Same Kind of Material?

Poor readers find comics and picture books more stimulating than most other reading material. In a sense, this is unfortunate because in today's information-oriented society, there are so many books and other reading matter to choose from. By reading new books for just fifteen minutes a day, a person can read about two per month, perhaps as many as twenty a year. That means he could read nearly 1,000 or more in his lifetime. But because the poor reader has limited his interests he is missing the greatest opportunity to read and to learn more that has existed at any other time in history. Don't be one of those poor readers who are missing the kaleidoscope of entertaining and highly informative reading.

The Key to Improving Your Reading

It is easy to turn poor reading habits into good ones. Like most study skills, however, reading takes practice. Begin by reading easy material faster and with a particular purpose in mind. Get actively involved in the reading process by mentally questioning what your author is trying to say. You will more likely be able to discover the main ideas and supportive details by developing an inquiring mind. Also, improve your reading rate for better comprehension. Tell yourself that you are are going to read the next assignment in exactly twenty minutes—and then do it! Not only will your comprehension improve, but you will increase your vocabulary by understanding more words from their context clues. Increase your reading speed whenever you can, slowing down only when you are being introduced to new terms or unfamiliar concepts. Then, as soon as you become well acquainted with them, bring your reading rate back up to a faster than normal pace (approximately 300-600 words per minute).

Context

As you read your assignments, follow these suggestions to help you get the ideas straight in your mind:

• Be certain that you understand the sentences you are reading.
If you don't, you may need to get help. Remember, the sentence is the context for those new words and concepts that are being presented. Don't read them without gaining some understanding.

• Watch for familiar words shifting from one part of speech to another, and from one meaning to another.
Just when you think you know the meaning of a word, someone comes along and changes it or modifies it a little. So, BE ALERT! Integrate contextual meanings into those meanings you have already learned. Expand your word power by learning to be flexible as you adjust your thinking to ever-present changes in word usage.

• Constantly ask yourself: "What did I just read or learn?"
Let your inquisitive mind, your enthusiasm and interest, keep you one step ahead of your reading. Think actively about what you are reading by asking questions such as "Are these good ideas?" and "What is the author going to say next?"

Comprehension

By concentrating more on new words and new ideas, you begin to gain a fuller understanding of your reading material. And as you read more critically you will build better habits of reading that will also help you to 'read between the lines,' gaining insight into the implications of the author. Your reading will go more smoothly, becoming more pleasurable and less frustrating.

Speed-Read Whenever Possible

Begin by reading a book or magazine for two minutes. Then, count the number of pages you have read. Now, take another two minutes and try to read twice as much without losing comprehension. To do this you must overcome two poor reading habits you may have. First, do not pronounce each and every word as you read. That will just slow you down. Second, break the habit of using a pencil or your finger to point to words. Instead, force your eyes to see a half a line of print at a time. You can do this easily with a little practice. In this way, your comprehension of what you read will increase, your time for reading will decrease, and more will be recorded and stored in your brain for future recall.

Scan and Skim Your Reading

Many students believe that their task is completed when they have read the last word in the chapter. Not true! At that point a good reader takes a few extra minutes to go back over the chapter, scanning and skimming to reinforce the author's main points. This will help you become more alert to your reading as you connect ideas together to remember how they fit into the whole picture.

Before you begin reading through your assignment page by page, scan through the chapter to find important ideas, names, dates, distances, prices, formulas, and other key concepts. Familiarize yourself with where the author has placed the information and in what order his ideas are presented.

Like scanning, the review technique of skimming will help you find the facts you need to know when you study for a test. Look at chapter titles, subheadings, charts and graphs for main ideas. Read the first and last sentences of each paragraph. These are generally where you will find key concepts and main ideas. Write down the page numbers and key words as you skim for later reference. Finally, determine how difficult the reading will be and how slowly you will have to read in order to understand the chapter.

Once you have mastered these reading techniques, you will see a real improvement in your understanding of what you read, an improvement in your grades, and an increase in your desire to explore a variety of subjects using your new reading skills.

Study Technique for Reading Assignments

1. Know exactly what your purpose is for reading the assignment.
2. Begin and end your reading by scanning and skimming.
3. Overview each paragraph by reading only the first and last sentences.
4. Look at the titles, subheadings, words in boldface type, and other key words and phrases to get an idea of the difficulty of the material.
5. Set a time limit for completing the assignment.
6. As you read, ask yourself, "What did I just read?" This will become more automatic and more motivating, the more actively you learn to read.
7. Always strive to read at a faster rate.
8. When you finish reading, go back, scan and skim to reinforce ideas you have read.

The Key to Improving Your Reading

Become as familiar with your reading assignments as possible. You don't jump into cold and unknown waters! In the same way, don't start reading without a purpose or without knowing what your assignment is all about. Once you have some familiarity with your material, go ahead and work through your assignment using this study technique for your reading. This will not only help you cut your study time in half, but you will learn twice as much in the process.

Well, now it's up to you. Take another short break. Then go back and review what you have learned in this chapter. When you feel you understand how to handle your reading with more expertise, try using these skills on your next assignment. Practice them and refine your study habits so that your learning experiences make more sense.

Study Warm-Ups

My Reading Log

Record new words, facts, and concepts you come across while you are reading your next assignment.

Title of Book/Chapter:_____ Date Read: _____
What I Learned: _____
_____
_____

Title of Book/Chapter:_____ Date Read: _____
What I Learned: _____
_____
_____

Title of Book/Chapter:_____ Date Read: _____
What I Learned: _____
_____
_____

Title of Book/Chapter:_____ Date Read: _____
What I Learned: _____
_____
_____

Reading Nonfiction

The subject of this reading assignment is: _____

A) Scan and skim through the pages quickly and then write down three questions that you will want to find the answers to:

Question #1: _____
Question #2: _____
Question #3: _____

B) Next, write down three interesting facts you found while scanning:

Fact #1: _____
Fact #2: _____
Fact #3: _____

C) After scanning, summarize the author's main ideas:

_____
_____
_____

D) Write down all new words you read in the assignment and then write down a short definition of each:

New Word	*Definition/Synonym*
_____	_____
_____	_____
_____	_____
_____	_____

Reading Fiction

Use this STUDY WARM-UP to find out how much you understand after reading a short story or novel.

Title:_____Author:_____Copyright_____
What is the theme or plot of this story? _____
_____

When and where did this story take place? _____

_____

Describe the main characters:

Main characters   *Description*

_____   _____

_____   _____

_____   _____

How did this story begin? _____

_____

How did this story end? _____

_____

What part of this story do you remember best? _____

_____

Write down three words that were unfamiliar to you. Define them.

_____   _____

_____   _____

_____   _____

Would you recommend this story to someone else? _____

Locating Main Ideas

Did you know that reading, outlining, and problem-solving skills all depend on how well you understand the relationships between the author's main ideas? It's true! So, always look for transitional words to help you connect them. That way you will be able to discover the organizational pattern used in your reading.

This assignment deals mainly with: _____

1. The first major idea is _____

    _____

    A) For example, one fact expressed concerns _____

    _____

    B) The author also suggested _____

    _____

2. Another major idea highlighted by a subhead is _____

    _____

A) A key word or phrase and its meaning are _____

_____

B) One specific fact the author emphasized is _____

_____

3.   The author's last major idea is _____

_____

A) One fact related to this last major idea is _____

_____

B) The last paragraph points out _____

_____

Speed-Read: The Challenge

1.   Using your favorite magazine, and giving yourself a three-minute time limit, speed-read every page, cover to cover. Look, concentrate, and try to remember what you see as you turn the pages at a faster than normal rate..

2.   Concentrate on the colorful pictures, article titles, boldface and unusual text, and whatever else flashes to mind as you scan.

3.   When three minutes are up, stop. Close the magazine and set it aside (whether you have gone all the way through it or not).

4.   Now, write down a list of words and phrases that stuck in your mind as you went through the magazine. Go ahead. Write down as many items as you can recall without looking back at the magazine. Give yourself three minutes to make this list.

5.   Repeat steps 1 to 4 to see if you can come up with a longer list the second time around.

6.   Compare the two lists. Which is longer? How many items did you write down for each list? All together, in only twenty minutes?

Each time you attempt this STUDY WARM-UP, try to 'top' your best score (the list with the most items). Then, just for fun, challenge someone to remember more than you. See who wins. Use this activity whenever you are about ready to tackle a class reading assignment. You will begin to improve your reading rate and study habits quickly.

CHAPTER VII

Organizing Your Writing

THOUGHT: Any man who will look into his heart and
honestly writes what he sees there, will find plenty
of readers.

Ed Howe

Do you have difficulty when it comes to writing assignments?
Almost everyone can improve his or her writing skill by following
these simple strategy tips:

1. Be brief but not too brief.
2. Choose your words with care.
3. Define key words that you use.
4. State your ideas in an objective manner.
5. Be concise, avoid abstractions.

Your ideas will flow more smoothly if you learn to lead your
reader through your written thoughts cogently, using a clearly defined
format or organizational pattern. In this way, you will be more
sensitive to the way you use the language, you will become more
concerned with your reader's expectations, and you will gain a
stronger sense of accomplishment.

Make one of your study goals to write the kinds of pertinent
information you know your reader will understand and appreciate.
In general, he will look for your introductory ideas at the beginning
of your writing, more specific details, examples, and other substantiating data in the main body of your text, and a summation of major
ideas in your concluding paragraphs.

Is writing all that simple? Well, no! But all too often, students
make their writing assignment more complicated than it needs to
be. Some just can't seem to get started. So, let's start at the beginning
and see what ideas go in what section of your writing: the introduction, body, and conclusion.

Introduction

Strive to accomplish at least these two writing goals in your first several sentences: (1) catch your reader's attention and interest by stating your main idea with an interesting fact, statistic, or example that is related to your overall topic, and (2) point out how your reader is going to benefit from what you have to say. Give him one or two good reasons to read further about your main ideas. If you pique his interest here, chances are he will read amiably to the conclusion of your thesis. Remember, your reader will become interested only if he can see some organizational pattern along with some value in your writing. Achieve these two writing goals early and you will be on your way to creating a well-written composition.

Body

Here, the length of your writing will vary with the topic, the amount of research you have done, and/or the time you have to prepare your final draft. At any rate, one of your main concerns is to lead your reader along, idea by idea, in a clear and logical manner. Depending on your topic, you will want to organize your information using one of the following patterns:

- Chronological Sequence—a step-by-step approach.
- Spatial Sequence—ideas are in reference to some space.
- Cause-Effect Sequence—often used in scientific writing.
- Topic Sequence—used in many textbooks with subtopical headings.
- Problem-Solving Sequence—discussed later in more detail.

Using one of the above organizational patterns or sequences, your main job in the body of your writing is to express your ideas clearly. You may also want to use visual aids such as sketches, graphs, and charts to help your reader visualize your ideas. Be sure to explain such aids so that they reinforce your point effectively. You must also develop a positive attitude and a little confidence in yourself. Good readers can sense your attitudes through your style of writing, your word choice, and the inferential information that some notice when they 'read between the lines.'

Conclusion

You have two final goals to accomplish at this point: (1) leave your reader with what you feel are the main ideas and the important thoughts you have been writing about, and (2) wrap up any loose ends. Put your main ideas into perspective by once again telling your reader how he can benefit from what you have said on this subject. If your writing has been coherent and clear, he will respond favorably; if not your grade may be in jeopardy! Be careful: Your conclusion, or summary, if written poorly, can destroy all of your previous writing. For example, in many business communications, the function (or the bottom line) is to clinch a deal, sell a product, or establish a policy or agreement among concerned parties. Here, the conclusion is designed to generate goodwill and a call to action. In doing so, the reader knows what he is to say or do, business is conducted, and a profit is made in the process. So, follow the example of professional writers in business: Make your conclusions as meaningful and as effective as possible.

Special Kinds of Writings

Clear Explanations

Can you write directions for others to understand? Many students sit and stare at a blank piece of paper when they are given a writing assignment to explain a process or procedure. Think about the time you had to follow someone else's directions when you put that model together, or tried that new recipe, or when you got lost going to a particular locale. Get in the habit of writing clear, concise explanations. Overcome the weakness many of us have, giving vague or misunderstood directions. The following three guideposts, if followed carefully, can make the difference between a muddled, confusing composition and a clear and accurate exposition.

Make one point at a time. Keep your directions clear and simple. Put only one main point in each paragraph, and explain that point in reference to the reader's own background. Use reference points and landmarks you both can agree upon. Generally, put your first main step or direction in your opening paragraph. Then you can add more specifics to clarify the how and why of that step. When you have finished writing each step of your instructions in a similar way, go back and look for steps that might be illogical or out of order. Get rid of confusing words and phrases. Put yourself in the reader's position and think about how he will respond to each paragraph, sentence, word, or illustration that you have written.

Define your terms. Write out your first draft and don't worry about major errors such as spelling and punctuation. You will take care of them later. For now, concentrate on the organization of your ideas. Remember, use words that your reader can understand, ones that won't be misinterpreted. It is also important to remember that words you think of in one way may not always be meaningful to others in that same context. So, use short, concise definitions, synonyms, and examples whenever you give directions in writing.

Illustrate your main points in expository writing. Often, a reader will grasp an idea only after another more specific illustration is presented. For example, if your expository writing is about 'The Conditions of Africa,' you might define your use of 'condition' and give the specific illustration of how millions of people will die of starvation today, and again tomorrow, due to the undeveloped conditions of the area. Your purpose would be to help your reader visualize your main point by helping him picture in his mind what you are trying to say in your written communication. Always seek such clarification of abstract thoughts with concrete illustrations. Be alert to the overtones in your message and guard against being misinterpreted.

Revise your rough draft several times until your explanations are as clear as you can make them. You will know your writing is successful if someone can follow and understand what you have said. If not, your reader may lack the necessary background information needed to go from one main point or step to another. So, it's a good idea to take one last look at your final draft and anticipate any questions that might come up. For instance, ''How do I begin?'' ''What comes next? Why?'' and ''What is the outcome going to look like?'' are questions that might help you put your final paragraphs clearly in perspective for your reader.

Critical Writing

The purpose of critical writing assignments is to help you learn to evaluate books you have read or theatrical performances you have seen. To begin this writing task, you first need to jot down notes at the time you read the book or observe the performance. You will want to refer to them later as you write your impressions and evaluation. They will help you substantiate your opinions and thoughts in a more objective manner as you consider the positive and negative aspects of your subject. If you have reliable notes to draw your thoughts from, chances are your descriptive writing will be both accurate and fair.

By critically describing the interesting and uninteresting parts of your subject, you will demonstrate your ability to express your criticisms in an unbiased way, using sound reason and judgment. Your teacher will prefer this approach to simply presenting trivial commentary that is shallow and not well thought out. So, carefully explain the weaknesses and strengths of your subject. Include suggestions as to how those weaknesses might have been handled more effectively. Compare and contrast other parts of your subject showing their relationship to one another as well as to their function or purpose.

Persuasive Writing

In some writing assignments, you are asked to persuade or convince your reader to buy a product or to agree with a point of view. You may be required to show good cause for contributing time and money to an organization or a movement. Begin your writing by showing your reader that you are a credible writer on the subject at hand. A good opening paragraph should show:

— the importance of accepting your ideas as being beneficial;
— a sincere concern for your reader's welfare;
— a friendly rather than an aggressive relationship;
— that you are competent and in command of the major issues.

Once these personal factors are established, you must use logic and sound reasoning in your effort to change your reader's attitude or feelings. Your writing must show how your ideas are important to your reader. And thus, he must be made to feel that he can trust you, that you have his good will in mind, and that by accepting your arguments or reasoning he will be better off. If you have done all of that throughout the body of your composition, your conclusion will include a plan of action that the reader will agree with and follow. Let him know what he should do once you have convinced him of your point of view. Explain how he can change his attitude or behavior with a minimum of effort and a maximum of benefit derived from that change.

In sum, help your reader understand your ideas by using words accurately and by presenting your ideas in a logical, organizational format. In short, state your main ideas in complete sentences and then develop those ideas with clear definitions and specific data so that he will be able to interpret your words in the way you intended them to be understood.

You are now on your way to becoming a more proficient writer, one who is able to control language more effectively, and one who can identify the purpose of a writing assignment and fulfill the reader's expectation.

A Writing Formula for Short Reports

The following writing formula will get you started on the short term reports your teacher assigns. Gather as much information beforehand as possible. Use both primary (first-hand) information gathered from observation, surveys, and interviews, and secondary (library research) data including material gathered in your notes from periodicals and books read on the subject you are reporting on.

As you begin to actually write your rough drafts, you might want to answer some of the following questions:

Introduction	What is the main purpose of writing?
	What are the main points I want to present?
	What organization pattern should I use?
	Why should my reader care about this topic?
Body	What are the most important ideas first?
	What details will clarify my ideas?

What are interesting points to include?
How can the reader relate my ideas to what he already knows?
What transitions (words/phrases) should I use to lead my reader from one point to another?

Conclusion   What are the main points I have made?
What should my reader do now that he has this information?
What alternatives might he consider?
What is the last thought I want to leave with my reader?

Use this formula to write and revise your short reports. Then, when you feel you have written your final draft, proofread for (1) flow of ideas, (2) punctuation, (3) spelling errors, (4) grammar, and (5) word usage. The more revisions you make, the more mistakes you will catch, and the better your writing will be.

Inductive and Deductive Writing

Another approach to writing assignments is to use inductive reasoning. Here, begin by writing down specific data such as examples, statistics, and other supportive details. By doing this first, you justify what will ultimately be your main point stated in your conclusion. Your job is to prove your point logically with substantiating evidence and facts presented before you state your thesis or main idea, leading your reader along so that he will see your case unfold in an orderly fashion and come to the same conclusion you have.

In deductive writing, you state your main point first. In essence, you take a stand. This is analogous, for example, to the courtroom lawyer who makes an opening statement telling the jury that his client could in no way be guilty of the crime of which he is accused. Then, he proceeds by calling witnesses and entering evidence to justify his stand. You, like that lawyer, have the job of 'backing up your words' with sound evidence and reasoning. Here is another example: If you begin your writing by telling your reader that Americans are worse off than they were four years ago, you had better be prepared to back up those words with some hard evidence pointing out the high unemployment rate, the burdens of having a federal deficit to contend with, and any other persuasive argument you can find to support your stand.

Journalistic Writing

One of the best approaches newspaper and magazine writers have found for expressing their ideas in publication is to organize their copy around a set of predetermined questions, questions they know their readers want answered. You may want to work through your next writing assignment in this fashion by considering these

Six Interrogatory Pronouns

WHAT
　What is my topic about?
　What is the most significant aspect of this topic?
　What does my reader really want to know about this topic?

WHY
　Why is this topic timely?
　Why does my reader care?
　Why did this event take place?

WHEN
　When did this happen or when did it have the most significant impact?
　Is this time frame (past, present, future) an important consideration?

WHERE
　Where did this event take place?
　Where has this event occurred before?
　Where does this topic/event affect others?

WHO
<u> </u>
Who are affected?
Who are immediately involved?
Who are responsible for what has occurred?

HOW
<u> </u>
How important or significant is this topic/event?
How will this event be viewed by others?
How should this event be explained or described?

Journalists all over the world record current events by addressing these and similar questions. They, like many other students of written communication, have learned to write their ideas clearly and succinctly in this manner. They have taken the advice of Rudyard Kipling in *The Just-So Stories:*

> I keep six honest serving-men
> (They taught me all I knew);
> Their names are What and Why and When
> And How and Where and Who.

The next time you are given one of those impossible writing assignments, use this approach. It will help you get to the heart of your composition more easily. Further, you will find that your ideas will fall into place more naturally. Practice writing with this approach and you will improve your natural ability to communicate and think using cause-effect relationships. By using this approach you will also be able to write about your subject with the other person's point of view in mind, tailoring your word choice and usage to a more appropriate style. You are now developing some expert skills used by professional writers.

Writing Analytical Reports

Whether your written reports are short or long, you must not only gather needed information through research, but you must also analyze the facts and write them down in a format that will help your reader understand the progression of your thoughts. This is not always an easy task. But when you consider a given topic in a problem-solution format, you may find writing a very logical process. More important, your reader will be able to follow your train of thought all the way through your report without being sidetracked.

A Problem-Solution Writing Format

Step 1   *Define the problem (or subject area)*
Based on your library research and other investigation, write down the exact nature of the problem. Give your reader the necessary background information he needs to discover what significance your problem really has. Also, be sure to limit the problem by defining exactly what aspect you are dealing with.

Step 2   *Analyze your research data*
Write down in what ways the problem affects others. Further analyze your primary and secondary data so that all information is clearly understood by your reader. Include statistics, cost factors, policy changes, and other data that show the status or importance of the problem. Be unbiased and objective in both your analysis and your writing. Provide quotations and other specific information to substantiate your ideas.

Step 3   *Decide on possible solutions*
From your notes, pick out what you feel might be possible alternatives or solutions to the problem. Write down the advantages and disadvantages of each one. Try to discover the solution (or combination) that will solve your particular problem. Also, write down what you think might work — weigh the merits of these ideas.

Step 4   *Choose the best solution*
From the alternatives that you have investigated in Step 3, describe the one that you feel will work best. Justify your choice by explaining how this solution will solve the problem better, more inexpensively, causing fewer lay-offs, policy changes and so on.

Step 5 *Implement your solution*
Once you have made a sound case for your solution, dem-
onstrate exactly what is needed to implement your plan.
Show your reader how to begin solving the problem under
investigation. ALL IS LOST IF HE AGREES WITH YOU
BUT DOES NOTHING ABOUT IT!

Study Warm-Ups

A Problem-Solving Trial Run

Practice using the problem-solution writing format on your next
assignment. Fill in each step as accurately as you possibly can, after
you have discussed your problem and have done some research.

Step 1 State your problem clearly and concisely.
Problem: _____

Step 2 Analyze your problem. Why is it a problem?
Important Facts: _____

Step 3 List five possible solutions.

____ _____

____ _____

____ _____

____ _____

____ _____

Step 4 Choose the best solution and explain why and how it will
work.
Best Choice: _____

Workability: _____

Step 5 How can your solution be implemented step by step?
Step ___ _____
Step ___ _____
Step ___ _____

Who is affected? _____

What will be the cost? _____

Any new changes in policy? _____

Other: _____

List possible classes and topics for which you can use this type of writing:

Class Title   Topic

_____   _____

_____   _____

_____   _____

_____   _____

_____   _____

Writing Reports

1. Gather primary and secondary data through critical observation and thorough research.
2. Organize your data in an outline. Decide exactly what you want to say to your reader—write down your central idea.
3. Continue writing your first draft. Rewrite it at least twice. Be sure that you have explained your central ideas with specific information.
4. Proofread for spelling, grammar, and punctuation errors. Stay in complete control of your written thoughts and ideas, not vice versa!
5. Be neat! Remember, your writing is a reflection of yourself.
6. Finally, submit your written report with pride and confidence— on time.

What are the exact requirements for this report?

Report topic: _____

Length of report: _____

Footnotes:	Yes_____	No_____
Bibliography:	Yes_____	No_____
Title page:	Yes_____	No_____
Table of contents:	Yes_____	No_____
An appendix:	Yes_____	No_____

Any other requirements: _____

Date this report is due: _____

CHAPTER VIII

Gathering Information

THOUGHT: To be conscious that you are ignorant is a great
step to knowledge.

Disraeli

In gathering information, begin with what you already know about
the subject. You may possess more information than you realize;
then again, you may not.

After you have searched your own brain for information on the
topic that has been given you for an assignment, your next logical
step is to look for information where you know there is an abundance
of facts and ideas related to your assigned topic — the library.

The Library

Know what is available in your library. There, you will find books,
periodicals, cassette tape recordings, films, and other sources of
information. And the best part is it's all free! If you cannot locate
what you are looking for, ask the librarian where to find the information for your research topic. Then, find out how he or she can help
you develop your research skills. He will be glad to point out the
sections of the library that contain the fiction and the nonfiction
books.

Fiction books are usually found together in libraries that use the
Dewey Decimal System. They are generally shelved in alphabetical
order by the author's last name. *Nonfiction books,* on the other hand,
are categorized a little differently, using 'call numbers' instead of
an alphabetical arrangement. More specifically, nonfiction reading
materials are located not only by their call number but also by subject
matter. Learn the following classifications, which are used in most
school and public libraries:

000-099 GENERAL WORKS

Here you will find books on a wide range of subjects, such as almanacs, encyclopedias, general magazines, and bibliographies; also in this section are books on library science and journalism.

100-199 PHILOSOPHY

Here are books about various aspects of human thought, such as psychology, logic, and philosophy.

200-299 RELIGION

In this section are the books about religions of the world, the Bible, and theology.

300-399 SOCIAL SCIENCE

Look here for books that deal with social conditions, government, economics, law, education, and custom and folklore.

400-499 LANGUAGE

Here you will find an assortment of dictionaries, grammars, and books about language and usage.

500-599 PURE SCIENCE

Books that deal with mathematics, astronomy, physics, chemistry, biology, zoology, and other sciences can be found here.

600-699 TECHNOLOGY (APPLIED SCIENCES)

This section of the library contains books dealing with how human beings have used science to make a living or to improve living conditions; also such subjects as inventions, medicine, engineering, agriculture, pets, food, home planning, clothes, building, and business.

700-799 THE ARTS

Here you will find an abundance of reading material about music, landscaping, architecture, painting, sculpture, dance, photography, and recreation.

800-899 LITERATURE
Here are books about the literature of all countries, including such areas as poetry, drama, fiction, essays, speeches, and humor.

900-999 GEOGRAPHY, HISTORY AND TRAVEL
Here you will find books about history, geography, and travel, as well as biographies and autobiographies.

Ask questions if you can't find what you are looking for. Become familiar with the library policies, hours, check-out period, and regulations. Students find many helpful resources such as duplicating machines and typewriters that are available free or at a minimal cost. There are, of course, other valuable reference resources in the library.

The Card Catalog will tell you whether the library has the book you want and where it is located. The card catalog is your starting point for a research project; it will lead you to many references to the topic you are investigating.

The Reader's Guide to Periodical Literature is the best single source for references to current and past magazine and journal articles, which you can also locate in the library. It indexes the articles of well over 200 general and nontechnical periodicals, all published in the United States. Many libraries keep bound volumes going back as far as 1900.

Encyclopedias. As a researcher, one of your most valuable resources are the many encyclopedias in your library. Here you will discover background material for almost every subject imaginable. In addition, encyclopedias provide you with bibliographies and other references for further research.

Sources of Information

You can find a variety of researched information. Your primary data may be company records, original letters, diaries, or data collected from personal experiences and observation, interviews and surveys, and experimentation. Secondary data is information found in books, magazines, and journals, which we have just mentioned.

Primary data, however, consists of evidence and information that you develop yourself. So, let's see how primary data can be gathered and used in our research projects.

Personal Knowledge and Observation

You have a wealth of personal knowledge that you have accumulated over your lifetime. The problem is to recall accurately the relevant information that pertains to your research topic. It is especially important to draw upon knowledge that you as an active observer have recorded. Keep a notebook of personal experiences that you think are important, the kind that might be the substance of future school assignments.

As you record and research your data for any learning experience, cultivate persistence in your research efforts, and learn to develop research techniques that will help you communicate your ideas effectively. One of the most common errors of students is to give up on their ideas too soon. Use the following guidelines to look at daily events that are important:

• Place yourself in a position to observe accurately and to learn new information firsthand.
• Use precise words as you record your observations.
• Write your report as soon after your observation as possible.
• Put your ideas in a clear, objective, and meaningful context for others.

Interviewing and Surveys

Gather needed data from interviewing others. This can be a very useful way to research a topic that you have been assigned. If, for example, your teacher asks you to find information related to the trends of the stock market, you may want to interview an expert in that field, a stockbroker. He may help you increase your knowledge of certain aspects of the subject that you might not otherwise find in books or publications. This is an especially enjoyable way of gathering information if you like talking with interesting people.

But do your homework first! Know your assigned topic, and what questions you need answered beforehand. Then after you have prepared some well-thought-out questions, and have made an appointment with someone who is an authority on the subject, you will be ready to explore various ideas that are brought up during the interview.

When you begin the interview, establish a warm and friendly relationship with the interviewee at the outset. Let him know exactly who you are and what your purpose is in interviewing him. Then, let him do most of the talking. Ask your questions and intrude as little as possible. Remember, the purpose of the interview is for you to draw information from him, not the other way around.

As you proceed, listen attentively and accurately record your information. Use a tape recorder only with the interviewee's permission. Write a transcript of your conversation immediately following the interview while your impressions and thoughts are fresh in your mind. You would be well advised to provide your interviewee with a copy also. He may catch some errors and help you by clarifying points that are vague. In this way interviewing professional business people and experts in sports, law enforcement, education and other fields can be very satisfying and informative.

Gathering data from surveys is another research approach. It is similar to interviewing in that you must carefully prepare questions that will insure relevant response. In fact, surveys are usually based on specifically worded questionnaires that call for very specific answers. As a researcher, you can then calculate the number of times your question was answered in a certain way, i.e. by counting the "yes" or "no" responses to a question. But, when you prepare your questionnaire, keep the questions fairly brief to avoid exhausting the interviewees to a point where they answer carelessly or stop responding altogether.

Surveys, then, are tools to determine the responses of other people: voters, students, friends, and targeted groups. Your research topic could range from problems of employees' rights, taxes, the budget deficit, to nuclear expansion. Surveys may take the form of printed questionnaires or face-to-face or telephone interviews. No matter which survey technique you use, decide ahead of time how you will word your questions and who will be the representative group of people to respond to your questionnaire. Your results are referred to as a consensus or a tally. Don't be misled though. Your results may not prove anything conclusive. Instead, the data may only indicate a trend or tendency, rather than scientifically proving that something is or is not valid.

Experimentation

If you want to see how a group of people respond to a given 'controlled situation,' you are gathering data from experimentation. When we hear the word experiment, we often picture scientists in their laboratories observing mice running through mazes. But advertising agencies, businesses, and various social and political groups conduct experiments regularly as well, to test their ideas or products. Here again, you are gathering first-hand knowledge about what others think or how they respond to a particular set of circumstances.

If your assignment is to conduct such an experiment, first determine and systematically record the "baseline" or normally expected responses or behaviors to a given stimulus. Second, you must control all of the variables that may affect the outcome of your experiment. Finally, repeat it until you are able to compare and synthesize your results. Now, you are looking for valid and reliable results! Be in command of the total situation at all times. It is a rigorous and demanding way to gather information, but you will find the challenge and the results rewarding.

Study Warm-Ups

Getting to Know Your Library

Ask your librarian for a brief tour of the library and rediscover the variety of resources that are available.

A)   What three kinds of information are found in the card catalog?

1. _____

2. _____

3. _____

B) Explain how the books are arranged and classified.

_____

_____

C) After you have completed your library tour, answer these questions:

What magazines are available? _____

What audio/visual materials are available? _____

What section of the library will help you the most? _____

Why? _____

D) Interview your librarian. Write down three questions you want him or her to answer:

1. _____

2. _____

3. _____

Find out how your library can help you improve your study skills. Fill in the blank spaces with the titles, call numbers, and any personal notes as you explore each of the following sections of the library. Write down only the titles of books that appeal to you. Jot down a brief description of how each book might help you in your study sessions.

	Title	*Call Number*	*My Notes*
000-099	_____	_____	_____
100-199	_____	_____	_____

200-299	_____	_____	_____
300-399	_____	_____	_____
400-499	_____	_____	_____
500-599	_____	_____	_____
600-699	_____	_____	_____
700-799	_____	_____	_____
800-899	_____	_____	_____
900-999	_____	_____	_____

List five references sources that may be found in the library:

    1. _____

    2. _____

    3. _____

    4. _____

    5. _____

Can any of these be checked out? _____

Writing Questions for Interviews and Surveys

Pick a controversial topic or one assigned by your teacher. Then write five questions that you might want to ask each of the following targeted groups:

Employees working for the city

    Controversial topic: _____

1. _____

2. _____

3. _____

4. _____

5. _____

Law enforcement personnel

    Controversial topic: _____

1. _____

2. _____

3. _____

4. _____

5. _____

Employees in an employment agency

    Controversial topic: _____

1. _____

2. _____

3. _____

4. _____

5. _____

Let's Experiment!

Describe an experiment you have witnessed, or one that you plan to conduct yourself:

    What is the nature of the experiment? _____

    _____

    What equipment do you need to conduct the experiment? __

    _____

    What variables must be controlled? _____

    _____

    How many times must this experiment be repeated to get reliable data? _____

    _____

    What other considerations and criteria are involved? _____

    _____

Go to your school library and read a book or magazine that explains either a famous or a contemporary experiment that has had some impact on our society. What did you learn about this experiment? _____

_____

_____

_____

CHAPTER IX

Improve Your Communication Skills

THOUGHT: "When *I* use a word," Humpty Dumpty said, in rather a scornful tone, "it means just what I choose it to mean—neither more nor less."
"The question is," said Alice, "whether you *can* make words mean so many different things."
"The question is," said Humpty Dumpty, "which is to be master—that's all."

from Alice Through the Looking-Glass
by Lewis Carroll

The ability to communicate and to study are interrelated. The very process of learning anything must include our powers of observation and concentration as well as other receptive abilities. In fact, throughout our lives, we have used our communicative skills to gain knowledge and insight, learning facts and theories from authors, teachers, parents, and friends. And we continually learn new knowledge as we develop and refine our ability to communicate. But it is language that has become the single most important ingredient in our melting pot of interpersonal relationships and learning experiences.

Language Is

Language is at the heart of the communication process because it is this complex system that holds the meanings of our symbols and signals. We decode verbal and nonverbal cues and translate them into messages. These messages may be in the form of words in a speech, an actor playing a role, a mime acting without words at all, or a variety of other systems including braille, semaphore, and sign language, to mention just a few. Today, language presented through the mass media touches our lives more intimately than it ever has before. Home computers have become a popular way of transmitting our thoughts and ideas to people in our community and around the world. Here a whole new language must be integrated with our more familiar words and signals.

But no matter which language we use, we must adhere to rules that make its use meaningful to ourselves as well as to others. And there are several hundred languages in the world to choose from. Whether Chinese, Russian, English, German, American Indian, or even slang, we find a structured set of rules to transfer meaning. Familiar words in our own language like 'freedom,' 'peace,' and 'goodwill' are deeply embedded and very useful. Other words such as 'hep,' 'far out' and 'that's boss' come and go as fads.

Language Is Based on Experience

A fable is told about a small child who set out one day to learn the meaning of each and every word ever uttered on earth. His aim was to possess all the knowledge in the world, for to know all is surely the one great purpose in life—right?

Well, after eighty years the child grew into a very old man—a very dismayed human being he was indeed.

There were untold thousands of words he had never studied, never discovered, and never understood. Then one day, Death came to the old man's bedside.

Death. Now, there is a word that everyone must experience. But before the old man passed on, his strained, whispery voice was heard in the darkened room, where his wife sat near a small flickering candle. ''Wife, what means this word Death?'' And without another whisper, they both knew. The candle went out as the wife sat and wept.

The moral: Words are empty vessels until we fill them with meanings gained from our experiences. They carry our sorrows and our joys, our knowledge and ignorance. They are the basis for the language we use to express our ideas to others.

Perception

Perception is a word used to describe the total awareness of reality that lies in our conscious mind. Selective perceptions are those experiences and events that we interpret as most meaningful. We gather up all the things we know with the only five learning tools we have, our five senses: hearing, feeling, tasting, smelling, and seeing. The brain is continually recording our experiences whether we are conscious of them or not. But, there are so many people with so many different perceptions of what is going on around them; it is a wonder we are able to communicate and agree on what we perceive at all. Take Camilia and Murtle for instance.

These two ladies were staring daggers at each other across the table in a quaint corner restaurant, one cloudy afternoon.

"Cam," Murtle huffed, "don't you think I know what I see? I still have better eyesight than you have!"

"A pig's eye!" Camilia snapped back. "Why, it's as plain as the nose on your face. That really is a beautiful picture of flowers hanging on that wall over there. And they are just lovely."

"Lovely, yes!" retorted Murtle irately, "but that picture just happens to be of beautiful butterflies fluttering about."

"Beautiful flowers," Camilia insisted.

"Beautiful butterflies," argued Murtle in a little louder tone of voice than she had intended.

Several customers heard their argument and became a bit annoyed. Finally the manager of the restaurant came to the table where they sat.

"Perhaps I can settle this argument," he said in a low whisper.

"Ladies, if you will please be kind enough to trade places, you will see what I mean."

Camilia and Murtle looked a little puzzled at one another. Then Camilia shrugged her shoulders, and the two ladies exchanged seats.

"You see," explained the manager, "if you view the picture on the wall from this side of the table, it does, indeed, look like a bouquet of lovely flowers. But now, if you sit on the other side, the picture appears to be one of beautiful butterflies. It all depends on your point of view."

Needless to say, Camilia and Murtle, a bit embarrassed by the whole affair, resolved their differences and thanked the manager.

As the sun peeked through the clouds outside, the two ladies were about ready to order a piece of marble cake. But they couldn't decide whether the cake was chocolate with vanilla filling or vice versa. They did agree on the number of calories that they would have to lose, tomorrow!

When we first perceive something that is new to us, we internalize it in a Gestalt manner. That is, we perceive what is new indiscriminately. But as we become more and more familiar with the individual components or factors of a new situation or event, we gain a different, more detailed perspective. Still, we tend to remember those details that are most meaningful to us and to our own particular viewpoint. Nevertheless, it is these same perceptions on which we base our ideas, and our language helps us to communicate what we have experienced, accurately or otherwise.

Messages

Communication may be defined as a sender (or transmitter) sending a message to a listener (or receiver), who in turns responds back to the initiator of the message. Although this is an oversimplication of the communication process, we can readily identify what is happening when one person communicates for the express purpose of giving information, to entertain, or to persuade his listener. The message is encoded by the sender and decoded by the listener based in part on common experiences and agreed upon usages of words.

The message is one of four major elements in the communication process that is designed to help us convey our ideas with well-chosen words. In fact, there are approximately 750,000 words to choose from in our English language today. We mentioned in Chapter V that the number of words an educated adult uses in daily conversations (not including technical jargon) is less than 1,000. Of these, as few as 500 words are used most frequently, and these have over 14,000 distinct dictionary definitions. The core unit then of a meaningful message are words, words which both sender and listener understand and interpret based on common experiences they share.

Channel, Receiver, and Response

The other three important elements in the communication process are channel, receiver, and response. The channel of communication is the means by which we convey messages, usually through oral and written media. The receiver of a communique may be called a listener, a reader, or perhaps a member of an audience. He is the recipient for whom the message was originally designed. As the initiator of that message, your responsibility is to determine what effect your ideas will have on that receiver. And that reaction will, in turn, be a factor that affects the way you design future messages. Response, or feedback, is the reaction you get from your message. By consciously revising your communication strategy, you will become a more interesting and more intelligent communicator. The more you are able to utilize the elements of communication, the more you will be able to improve on your own speaking and listening abilities along with improving your study skills generally.

Listening

As early as 1940, Dr. Goldstein completed a very important bit of research at Columbia University. The study was designed to compare the relative efficiency of reading and listening—the two media through which we do most of our learning. Two major observations may be gleaned from this research. First, it has become evident that we are able to listen to human speech at more than three times the speed at which we normally hear it without any loss of comprehension. Second, it is a bit unsettling to discover that we have not given much attention to the area of listening training along with teaching people to read. The research concludes that the public schools should place more emphasis on developing this vital skill at a very early age.

Richard Hubbel, another researcher, declared that 98 percent of all that a person learns in his lifetime is learned via the eyes and ears.

Still another researcher, Paul Rankin from Ohio State University, asked 65 white-collar workers to keep a careful log of all communication during their waking daytime hours at 15-minute intervals. After tabulating their data he found some very interesting characteristics in their communication.

He concluded that 70 percent of our waking day is spent in some form of communication. Seven out of every ten minutes that we are conscious, we send or receive messages. Rankin categorized the four components of communication in this way: We spend 9 percent of our communication time in writing, 16 percent in reading, 30 percent in speaking and 45 percent in listening.

There has been strong emphasis in recent years on developing better listening skills. Today, many corporations and both public and private educational institutions offer various kinds of listening programs. In addition, governmental agencies and every branch of the military service currently provide such training programs for selected personnel.

A good deal of your time is probably spent inside a classroom, presumably listening to what your teacher(s) have to offer. Teachers must repeat their instructions half a dozen times before the majority of a class fully understand exactly what is called for in a given assignment. And listening and following directions has become an impossible task for some. A few students never really catch on to the art of listening for key concepts, test question clues, or important terminology and ideas. So, you will be further ahead if you follow these simple guidelines:

1. Decide that the subject you are listening to is interesting.
    Good listeners develop an interest in what they listen to. They sift and screen all ideas that come their way. Remember, there are no uninteresting subjects, just uninterested people.
2. The key to listening effectively is concentration.
    Good listeners develop the ability to ignore distractions by taking notes and concentrating on what is being said. Rather than daydream, they keep their thoughts in line with what the teacher is teaching.
3. Wait until all the facts have been presented.
    Good listeners withhold evaluation of what they are listening to until they fully comprehend it, or until they have given the speaker a fair chance to be heard.
4. Develop a fact-finding attitude.
    Good listeners listen carefully to everyone's ideas. Facts make sense only when they can be substantiated by specific details. Learn to be an 'idea' listener and you will have developed a unique skill in your STUDY STRATEGY.
5. Anticipate the speaker's next thoughts.
    Good listeners are active listeners, mentally putting the pieces of the puzzle together and finding new relationships. Compare and contrast the ideas under discussion; anticipate the direction the speaker is taking. That will keep you a step ahead.
6. Mentally review and ask questions.

Interact in the learning experience—jot down notes, make outlines, and ask questions. This will give you better understanding of the overall topic.
7. Make the learning of difficult concepts a challenge.
Instead of faking attention, fantasizing, or bowing to distractions, intensify your efforts, concentrate on abstract concepts and technical terms with which you are not familiar.

Listening Is More Than Hearing

Poor listeners think that they are listening when they are really only hearing sounds. Hearing is not always listening! Hearing is the physical ability to receive sounds through sound waves that bombard us every day of our lives. Further, we are unable simply to turn our hearing on or off. That's why you may wake up in the middle of the night thinking you have just heard a dog barking or some strange noise coming from outside. Unlike listening, hearing is a passive, continuous process similar to breathing and blinking. Listening, on the other hand, is an activity that takes a real conscious effort, and more energy on our part. Listening involves actively concentrating on those sound waves that may hold meaning for us. Here, we pay attention to verbal messages, which must be decoded and then stored in the brain for future reference.

Be an Active Listener

In summary, there are several ways you can develop better listening skills right now. First, be sensitive to all kinds of sounds in your immediate environment, screen out those that are distracting, and concentrate on the ones that are important. Learn new ideas by telling yourself that you are going to become more interested in whatever you listen to. Do this by becoming actively involved: Pay attention, concentrate, take careful notes for later reference. Put that little extra energy into the listening process and you will come away with more understanding and a lot less frustration.

Ignore all distractions and follow the speaker's train of thought. If you will set your mind to the task in this way, you will be surprised at how much more enjoyable classroom activities and other learning experiences can be.

Study Warm-Ups

Better Ways to Communicate

Here are ten ways you can become a better communicator:

1. Have confidence in yourself and in your ability to communicate.
2. Be honest and sincere.
3. Use simple, unpretentious language.
4. Listen more than you speak.
5. Choose your words carefully—say what you mean.
6. Talk to others in the same way you expect them to talk to you.
7. Use sound reasoning.
8. Find the other person's point of view.
9. Be prepared to accept the consequences of your own communication.
10. Communicate so that others may know your true self.

Now it's your turn. List ten ways you can improve your own communication behavior:

1. _____
2. _____
3. _____
4. _____
5. _____
6. _____
7. _____
8. _____
9. _____
10. _____

Demanding Sound Signals

Make a list of twenty objects, machines, and names of people to whom you must listen throughout your daily routine. Place a (+) if you enjoy listening or a (−) if you do not enjoy listening to them:

1. _____   11. _____
2. _____   12. _____
3. _____   13. _____
4. _____   14. _____
5. _____   15. _____
6. _____   16. _____
7. _____   17. _____
8. _____   18. _____
9. _____   19. _____
10. _____   20. _____

Which of these sounds should you listen to more carefully? __
_____

Keep a "listening log" for one month. Record all the things you listen to and why. Record the date and then add at least one full page of details describing your listening events and how you feel about each of them. Try to discover new patterns and techniques that will help you improve your listening ability.

Listening to Directions

Practice listening more carefully to directions. Have someone give you four or five specific instructions to follow. Write them down accurately and then follow each instruction a step at a time. Keep the following daily log to help you record your progress:

		Direction Log	
Date	*Kind of Direction*	*Followed*	*Not Followed*
_____	_____	_____	_____
_____	_____	_____	_____
_____	_____	_____	_____
_____	_____	_____	_____

Date	Kind of Direction	Followed	Not Followed
___	___	___	___
___	___	___	___
___	___	___	___

Which directions are the most difficult for you to follow? Why? _
_____

What is one way you can improve your ability to follow these kinds of directions? _____

Each day challenge yourself to follow all directions given to you. Each day meet that challenge to the best of your ability.

Sound Listening

1. Take a minute to sit down and listen to all the sounds that are around you. Sit comfortably, close your eyes, and just listen.
2. Next, take another minute and write down what you heard:

    _____   _____
    _____   _____
    _____   _____
    _____   _____

3. Now, write down how you felt while you were listening to those sounds: _____
    _____

4. On another piece of paper, write a story entitled "My Most Ridiculous Tale." Use the above sounds for a springboard— write about whatever pops into your head. Describe the sounds and your feelings as you make up a crazy story. Have fun! Make up a strange tale that may make sense, may not.
5. (Optional)
    A. Mail your tale to a friend.
    B. Use a tape recorder and in an announcer's voice read your tale.
    C. Draw a sketch depicting the theme at the end of your tale.
    D. Read your tale to someone and watch his reaction.

Sound off! Let your imagination run wild for a while. You will enjoy studying a lot more when you set some time to practice your own unique brand of creativity.

Preparing Your Oral Report

1. First know the purpose of your oral report (to inform, entertain or persuade).
2. Gather a minimum of four interesting and informative facts related to your report.
3. Write each of these facts neatly on 3 x 5 notecard. Then add one specific idea, example, statistic, or illustration to each card.
4. Next, arrange your notecards in a logical sequence (i.e., from most important to least important ideas, etc.).
5. Number your notecards.
6. Practice your report aloud, referring to your notecards but not reading word for word. Rather, paraphrase your thoughts in a conversational manner, practicing good posture and using gestures naturally. Also, maintain eye contact by looking up as often as possible.
7. As you practice stay within the allotted time given you to speak.
8. Adhere to all of the requirements of this oral assignment:
   Report topic: _____
   Time limit: _____
   Purpose of my report: _____
   My audience/evaluators: _____
   My first main point: _____
   My final main point: _____
   Other requirements: _____

Organize Your Speech Simply

Before we begin putting your speech together, let's consider the following pre-planning questions:

To whom am I presenting my speech? _____
This question obviously requires a little reflective thinking about your intended audience. You would probably want to prepare an oral book report for English class a little differently than you would a report on a science project. If you are presenting an acceptance

of a student body office to a school assembly, that too takes careful preparation. So, decide at the outset who, if anyone, will be evaluating or grading your speaking abilities, and then plan your speech around their expectations.

What is the value of my speech? _____

What do you intend to accomplish with your speech? Are you going to persuade your audience to accept your point of view? Is your intent simply to inform or to entertain them? As you begin to gather information for your speech, you will want to decide exactly what information will be interesting, informative, and timely.

What is the point of your speech? _____

The answer to this question will determine just what kind of response you expect from your audience at the conclusion of your speech. Try to anticipate their questions and feedback whenever possible. Plan to leave your audience with the major point of your speech as you conclude your presentation.

So, remember, research your topic well, organize your information on 3 x 5 notecards in a logical manner, and then practice your speech aloud at least half a dozen times. Be confident. Be relaxed, and be friendly.

Begin your speech preparation by filling in this preliminary data sheet.

What is my speech topic? (Be specific) _____
_____

What is my first main point? _____
_____

What is a specific related idea? _____
_____

What is my second main point? _____
_____

What is a specific related idea? _____
_____

What is my third main point? _____

_____

What is a specific related idea? _____

_____

What is my final main point? _____

_____

What is a specific related idea? _____

_____

Write down three 'follow-up facts' or ideas that you can add during your question-answer period (Use quotations, statistics, examples, etc.):

    1. _____

    2. _____

    3. _____

Now you are ready to transfer the above information onto your notecards.

CHAPTER X

Preparing For Group Discussion

THOUGHT: An error of opinion may be tolerated where
reason is left free to combat it.

Thomas Jefferson

Group discussion refers to two or more people exchanging ideas
in some systematic manner (usually with the use of an agenda),
with specific goals and objectives in mind. This may include gathering ideas, presenting information, and solving problems. But in
order for people to get together in groups and achieve desired goals,
there is one important factor needed: a high degree of cohesiveness.
Without it very little will be accomplished because of a lack of
cooperation and earnest participation.

Types of Groups

Study Groups

Study groups or learning groups are formed by three or four
students for the purpose of coming together and sharing their knowledge on a particular subject, which they can learn better through a
collective effort. As these students interact in their discussion, they
gain valuable insight from many different angles. Furthermore, they
are able to practice their communication skills that are related to
speaking, listening, and critical thinking.

Brainstorming

This type of discussion is used in business, industry, and education.
The primary purpose of brainstorming is to amass a large quantity

of original ideas. Here there is no room for criticism or for any kind of negative evaluation concerning the ideas expressed. The more freewheeling and spontaneous the suggestions are, the better. During this discussion a participant is designated as the recorder. His task is to transcribe the ideas that are presented and discussed. Afterward, they are screened and passed along for further investigation and discussion by other groups or individuals, whose task is to decide how feasible the ideas may be, and the best way to implement them.

The Symposium/Forum

The two discussions mentioned above are private discussions; there is no audience to interact with the members of the groups. The symposium is specifically designed to present from four to ten speakers who are experts in their field. Each of these participants is given equal time to present new ideas before an audience. For example, a local law enforcement agency may sponsor such a group discussion to inform the general public about child abuse, drug prevention programs available in the community, or other issues of major concern.

During this more formal setting, a moderator or group leader first introduces the speakers and the topic they have been assigned to speak about. He summarizes each member's main points before going on to the next speaker. Then, at the conclusion of the symposium, the moderator conducts an informal open forum, or question-and-answer period. Members of the audience may ask for more information or further clarification on a point that a speaker made. Thus, the purpose of such a group discussion is not to solve a problem, but simply to disseminate information, dispel myths, and clarify issues under consideration.

Role-Playing (Therapy) Discussions

The purpose of a role-playing discussion is to explore theoretical situations that have been prearranged. Members assume a particular role and then act through a given situation. Dialogue is usually spontaneous and unrehearsed. For example, a teacher may want a class to investigate the value of being honest by asking one student to play the role of a person who observed another student cheating on an examination. The cheater receives an A +, the other student fails the test. The teacher may add another feature to this hypothetical scenario by suggesting that the 'cheater' is also the 'class bully.' Similar kinds of roles and situations are presented to scrutinize possible alternatives or decisions that may be resolved.

Problem-Solving Discussion

Most of us will be involved at some time in a problem-solving discussion, whether in a business meeting, a classroom activity, or a P.T.A. or other similar organizational meeting. The focus of the group members is on identifying a relevant problem. Often, the group objective is to find a workable solution agreeable to everyone involved in a difficult situation. This discussion is usually very structured, based on some modification of the reflective thinking process, which we will discuss shortly as a sound STUDY STRATEGY technique.

Participating in Groups

Communicate Constructively

You will encounter a good deal of interpersonal communication during your group discussion. You must learn to participate by seeking the opinions and ideas of others, by listening to what other people think is important, their beliefs and attitudes concerning discussion topics, as well as contributing your own ideas. Share in the group's efforts to achieve desired goals. Understand these goals and discuss them openly. Use appropriate language, as you contribute your ideas. Don't try to monopolize the discussion, but help maintain a balance of ideas for everyone to consider and evaluate.

Prepare Your Ideas in Advance

Know what the main topic will be, how much time will be allotted to each group participant, and exactly what role you are to play in the discussion. If you do not know much about the discussion topic, find out more by reading books and magazine articles, and by talking to friends and other group members. Be prepared to answer any questions that may arise during the discussion. In short, be prepared to participate. Show that you can discuss important information intelligently, accurately, and with sound reasoning. Also be willing to help others in your group clarify their ideas whenever necessary Be a supportive member in this way, by discussing important issues and facts that are related to the topic.

Compromise When Necessary

Often, conflicting viewpoints will surface, or a personality conflict may get in the way of the group's progress, resulting in polarization or hostility by other members. When such nonproductive situations arise, it is best to find common ground for agreement. Thus, it is in everyone's best interests to compromise and return once again to a more cooperative climate, at the same time reducing tension and frustration. Compromising is not giving in to someone else's point of view. It is simply a starting point for rebuilding the cohesiveness needed to help the group reach its intended objectives.

Maintain an Open Mind

Discussions are not always intended to be debates. It is tempting to think that this is your opportunity to prove a point or disprove some other person's ideas. But twisting the meaning of other people's thoughts and then restating those ideas inaccurately is often non-productive and wastes the time and energy of the group members. Instead of putting others on the defensive, encourage open-minded-ness, consider all new ideas fairly. Always attempt to create a pleasant, cooperative atmosphere for honest and objective discourse.

Tension is also found in groups where the participants become too serious, overly concerned, or just plain argumentative. When you notice this happening in your group, try a bit of humor. You can release tension by just sitting back for a moment and laughing at what may have been taken to a ridiculous point. Take your discussion seriously, but not too seriously. Create an environment that is conducive to a constructive and open exchange of ideas. To do this, you must learn to speak responsibly. Argue the validity of an issue but never argue the integrity of the member who holds that view. Be sure you understand what the other members are proposing before rejecting their ideas. Hear them out! Many arguments are easily resolved by simply trying to understand the other person's point. Define and redefine terms, clarify issues and facts that have been misinterpreted or misunderstood. Actively participate in a positive manner that will help the group achieve the established goals.

Four Major Group Roles

According to John Brilhart in his book *Effective Group Discussion*, group participants perform various functions during a discussion. One person may be assigned the role of initiator, another, information giver or information seeker. Still another major role is that of recorder. The following brief description will help you identify those fulfilling these roles:

Initiator. This person may begin the discussion by proposing group goals, defining limits or positions of group members in relation to their goals.

Information Givers. These participants may supply needed facts and information, or evidence for the group to consider.

Information Seekers. These participants ask questions and request information and further clarification of points under discussion.

Recorder. Often, someone is designated to keep minutes or factual records of what has been discussed. Later, this person may write a formal report of all the ideas and proposals of the discussion.

Evaluating a Group Discussion

What makes a good group discussion? Good question! It is one we need to answer in order to understand whether or not any goals were attained. Group discussions are considered effective if they satisfactorily solve an important problem or find an alternative to alleviate a crisis. Groups are also considered effective if they have given their audience enough information on which to base decisions. To fully analyze the productivity of a group, you might want to find answers to such questions as these: Did the discussion seem to be orderly and organized? Were the participants prepared? Did each make a significant contribution? Were all members given a fair amount of time to express their ideas? Were the group goals clear from the outset? Did everyone understand them? Was the leader helpful? Was the leader's role appropriate? Was the leader in control throughout?

How to Prepare for Discussions

Here is a five-step STUDY STRATEGY that will help you prepare for your next assigned group discussion:

1. Organize your thoughts.
    A. Take time to think about your assigned topic.
    B. Write down a list of your own ideas about your assigned topic.
    C. Organize your ideas in some logical sequence so that later you can connect those ideas with those expressed in the discussion.
    D. Rehearse your ideas point by point in a conversational manner.
2. Gather additional information for support.
    A. Prior to the discussion, add to your own ideas some research data that you can present as supporting your views.
    B. Remember to jot down sources of all quotable material.
3. Evaluate your information.
    A. Determine if your information fits logically into the discussion or if it is 'exception to the rule' information.
    B. Articulate your information fairly, concisely, and confidently.
4. Use the problem-solving format as your discussion outline.
    A. Help others define the problem (topic).
    B. Discuss the background of the problem.
    C. Point out solutions and alternatives.
    D. Help decide on a workable course of action.
    E. Devise plans to implement the group's solution.
5. Make last-minute preparations.
    A. Study your notes so that you will be able to adapt your information as different ideas are discussed.

B. Speak to your audience as well to the other group members as clearly as possible.

C. Present ample background information. Don't assume your audience knows more about the topic than they do.

Use this five-step strategy as you first become involved with group discussions. You will be able to prepare and present your ideas more effectively with this STUDY STRATEGY. It is an approach that can help you put your research and ideas together more concisely and help you to coordinate your efforts with those of the other group participants. Now, begin practicing these five steps by completing the following Study Warm-Up.

Study Warm-Ups

My Group Discussion Plan

What is the primary goal of this group discussion? ＿＿＿＿＿＿

＿＿＿＿＿＿＿＿＿＿＿＿＿＿＿＿＿＿＿＿＿＿＿＿＿＿＿＿

What is my assigned topic? ＿＿＿＿＿＿＿＿＿＿＿＿＿＿＿

＿＿＿＿＿＿＿＿＿＿＿＿＿＿＿＿＿＿＿＿＿＿＿＿＿＿＿＿

How much time will I have to present my ideas?

＿＿＿＿＿＿＿＿＿＿＿＿＿＿＿＿＿＿＿＿＿＿＿＿＿＿＿＿

＿＿＿＿＿＿＿＿＿＿＿＿＿＿＿＿＿＿＿＿＿＿＿＿＿＿＿＿

What three sources of information can I cite as references?
  1. ＿＿＿＿＿＿＿＿＿＿＿＿＿＿＿＿＿＿＿＿＿＿＿＿＿
  2. ＿＿＿＿＿＿＿＿＿＿＿＿＿＿＿＿＿＿＿＿＿＿＿＿＿
  3. ＿＿＿＿＿＿＿＿＿＿＿＿＿＿＿＿＿＿＿＿＿＿＿＿＿

What are three main points I want to make during this discussion?
  1. ＿＿＿＿＿＿＿＿＿＿＿＿＿＿＿＿＿＿＿＿＿＿＿＿＿
  2. ＿＿＿＿＿＿＿＿＿＿＿＿＿＿＿＿＿＿＿＿＿＿＿＿＿
  3. ＿＿＿＿＿＿＿＿＿＿＿＿＿＿＿＿＿＿＿＿＿＿＿＿＿

How much time will I have to prepare for this discussion? _____

_____

How can I best prepare for this oral assignment?

_____
_____

Who will be the leader or moderator of this group? _____

Who will speak   first? _____
                 Second? _____
                 Third? _____
                 Fourth? _____

When will I speak in this discussion? _____

What is the first thing I want to say? _____

What is the last thing I want to say? _____

Analyzing a Group Discussion

Listen to a tape recording of a group discussion. Then complete
the following:
What was the main discussion topic:? _____
What was the perceived purpose of this group?

_____

On a scale of 1 to 10, 1 = very poor, 10 = superior, how would
you rate this group's cohensiveness? Explain: _____

_____

Which participant sounds the most knowledgeable? _____

_____

How could this discussion have been made more interesting? _____

_____

Were most statements presented as facts or as opinions? _____

Give an example of a factual statement presented. _____
_____

What did you think of the way the leader handled the discussion? _
_____

How could the leader have been more effective?
_____

What were the leader's responsibilities? _____
_____

CHAPTER XI

Study Skills for Jobseekers

THOUGHT: The most reliable way to anticipate the future is by understanding the present.

from *Megatrend* by John Naisbitt

Do you have the study skills and business training to get the job you want? Do your vocational interests coincide with your potential for success? And how about your thinking abilities? Can you make that tough business decision when the situation demands it? Are you able to communicate your ideas and decisions effectively so that your co-workers will understand you?

These are only a few of the many questions employers want answered as they screen and interview prospective employees. They are interested in your educational background and your ability to gain the necessary experience from on-the-job training programs that many corporations now offer entry-level workers.

As a jobseeker entering or reentering the work force, you should plan to meet such expectations by developing the skills that will be needed to fulfill all job requirements. But we must first find out what your real interests and your skills are right now. Let's take a realistic approach by completing this Vocational Interest Inventory honestly and thoughtfully.

My Vocational Inventory

My name _____

My first choice for an occupation _____

Directions: Place a "1" before each of the following if you have a very positive reaction, a "2" if you have a neutral reaction, or a "3" if you have a very negative reaction toward the description.

_____ 1. Work with tools (power saw, drill, hammer, nails, etc.)
_____ 2. Work that necessitates manual skills
_____ 3. Work with computers or other electronic equipment
_____ 4. Work that necessitates some form of physical activity
_____ 5. Work outdoors
_____ 6. Work putting things together
_____ 7. Work that applies mathematical procedures and statistics
_____ 8. Work based on scientific procedures or data
_____ 9. Work that involves physical danger or risk
_____ 10. Work dealing with research and exploration
_____ 11. Work involved with buying and distributing materials or products
_____ 12. Work in a service area (church, hospital, welfare agency)
_____ 13. Work in which cooperation and courtesy are essential
_____ 14. Work that requires a great deal of traveling
_____ 15. Work requiring punctuality
_____ 16. Work requiring entertaining others
_____ 17. Working with a great deal of money (not your own)
_____ 18. Work involving leadership
_____ 19. Work in which you are directed or supervised
_____ 20. Work involving sharp or discriminating vision
_____ 21. Work involving rapid finger or hand movement
_____ 22. Work involving some kind of sport activity
_____ 23. Work involving a great deal of writing
_____ 24. Work in noisy surroundings
_____ 25. Work requiring considerable speaking
_____ 26. Work requiring ability to express ideas clearly
_____ 27. Work in an office
_____ 28. Work of an artistic nature
_____ 29. Work with soil and plants
_____ 30. Work with animals
_____ 31. Work involving listening and counseling others
_____ 32. Work that instructs and teaches people
_____ 33. Work exemplifying a high moral character

_____34. Work requiring systematic neatness and order
_____35. Work with office machines
_____36. Work correcting spelling, punctuation, use of words
_____37. Work cooking, sewing, or both
_____38. Work requiring technical knowledge and skills
_____39. Work requiring manipulation of information
_____40. Work demanding exceptional appearance

Now, let's take a look at all the items you mark as "1's." Can you find a commonality or pattern to your positive reactions? What three occupations can you think of that correspond to these reactions?

1._____   2._____   3._____

How do these compare with the occupation you chose initially, the one at the beginning of this inventory? Now, check your vocational interests.

My Vocational Interests

What occupation are you really most interested in? Check the ones below that you might like to investigate further. Place a double check (XX) by the ones that are especially interesting to you.

Outdoors
__Forest ranger
__Naturalist
__Farmer
__Sportsman
__Lifeguard

Mechanical
__Auto mechanic
__Watchmaker
__Computer technician
__Engineer
__Draftsman

Scientific
__Doctor
__Dentist
__Anthropologist
__Aviator/astronaut
__Pharmacist

Artistic
__Painter
__Sculptor
__Architect
__Photographer
__Decorator

Literary
__Writer
__Teacher
__Reporter
__Editor
__Correspondent

Musical
__Musician
__Singer
__Songwriter
__Music teacher
__Conductor

Persuasive
__Performer
__Politician

Social Services
__Nurse
__Minister

Clerical
__Computer operator
__Bookkeeper

___Radio announcer   ___Social worker   ___Secretary
___Insurance agent   ___Teacher   ___Stenographer
___Salesperson   ___Counselor   ___Bank employee

What is one major skill you have that will help you decide on a job?

Coping With Vocation Skills

The study skills that you have developed thus far will greatly enhance your chances for success on the job, especially those communication skills discussed in earlier chapters. One major prerequisite to entering the business world is to know the special language used on the job everyday. The jargon or 'shoptalk' that is often used in business becomes an integral part of an employee's thinking and communicative abilities as he goes about his daily routine. So, as you begin your new job, follow these guidelines to help you acquire this special language.

Look and Listen for New Terminology

Be alert to how co-workers express their ideas on the job. You may run into many technical terms as you enter a new occupation. Learn the meanings of these words by asking for clarification. Then, once you understand the terminology of your business, quickly incorporate it into your own expressive vocabulary. Once you can demonstrate your use of these words appropriately as you express your own business ideas, you become more intimately associated with others, and your ideas become more readily understood and accepted.

Write Down Difficult Terms

Many unique phrases and terms are used to refer to specific functions of machinery or services that may not be understood by the general public. These words should be used on the job when they are meaningful in specific situations. Often, they are difficult to learn, though. So, get into the habit of carrying a "Business Vocabulary Notebook," one that you can easily refer to and jot down difficult terminology that you must know. When you read or hear abstract words and ideas write them down and look them up in a dictionary at your earliest convenience.

Divide and Conquer New Terms

Many business dictionaries are available at your local bookstore. Find a pocket dictionary to carry with you if words are especially difficult for you to learn. Take a few minutes during your lunch break or after work to check the meanings and spellings of all business terms that you have heard or read during the day. Find a way to remember a new word; use synonyms or some memory association that will remind you of how the word is divided and spelled, its etymology, and how it is pronounced and used in that special business language.

Once you have learned these business terms, use them with confidence in your conversation and business writing. Your chances for business success and advancement will increase as you continue to improve your business and communication skills with persistence and determination.

So, let's get started. Begin your Business Vocabulary Notebook by writing all of the words below that you are uncertain about. These "must know" terms are used in many areas of government, business, and industry.

"Must Know Words" in the World of Business

Acceptable	Accommodate	Accomplish	Accurate
Bureau	Commission	Commodities	Deductible
Deficiency	Disbursement	Equivalent	Facilities
Feasible	Guarantee	Maintenance	Occupant
Management	Representative	Voluntary	Yield

Business worlds I am not certain about:

_____   _____   _____   _____

Job Jargon

Below write down three job-related words you have come across. Then write a synonym for each word:

_____	_____	_____
_____	_____	_____

Write these words in your Business Vocabulary Notebook and refer to them as often as necessary.

Also check the connotative as well as the denotative meanings of business terminology. Write down ten words that may elicit strong positive and negative reactions:

Job Jargon	*Positive Reaction*	*Negative Reaction*
_____	_____	_____
_____	_____	_____
_____	_____	_____
_____	_____	_____
_____	_____	_____
_____	_____	_____
_____	_____	_____
_____	_____	_____

Study Warm-Ups

Study the Job Market

Gather information related to job requirements, descriptions, and opportunities from public and private employment agencies, school counselors, college career centers, and from personnel offices of the businesses you are interested in. You will want to keep this information in an organized "Career Journal." Write down your ideas and all pertinent data related to potential employment opportunities for ready reference. Include copies of application letters, dates they were sent, and any other information such as résumés and sample work you have mailed along with your inquiries. You may want to begin your journal with the following:

Title of Job Opportunity_____Date_____
Required Skills for Job_____ _____
Education Needed to Apply_____
Background or Work Experience Required_____
Date I Mailed My Application___Date of Response___

Title of Job Opportunity_____Date_____
Required Skills for Job_____ _____
Education Needed to Apply_____
Background or Work Experience Required_____
Date I Mailed My Application___Date of response___

Finding the Right Job

It is not always easy to find the kind of job you want. You must have in mind more than one job for which you are qualified. Today, more than ever, new occupations are being created and old ones are becoming obsolete and nonexistent. Training and retraining for job changes has become a way of life for many of today's business people. You would be well advised to keep an eye on the classified sections of newspapers for these changes. Also talk with co-workers and keep in touch with your employment agency or personnel office for new openings.

Below, make a list of ten alternative occupations you might consider in the future. Next to each, jot down an important job skill required for each job.

	Occupations	*Job Skills*
1.	_____	_____
2.	_____	_____
3.	_____	_____
4.	_____	_____
5.	_____	_____
6.	_____	_____
7.	_____	_____
8.	_____	_____
9.	_____	_____
10.	_____	_____

My Vocational Data Sheet

Before you prepare a formal résumé for your next prospective employer, answer the following questions and see if you really qualify for the position.

My occupational goals are:
A) _____
B) _____
C) _____

My educational background includes:
A)_____   _____Date_____
B)_____   _____Date_____
C)_____   _____Date_____
(You need only go back five years)

My work experience includes:
A)_____   _____Date_____
B)_____   _____Date_____
C)_____   _____Date_____

Special (or needed) skills include:
A) _____
B) _____
C) _____

Other related experience or training includes:
A) _____
B) _____
C) _____

A Vocational Starting Point

For up-to-date data about specific careers and business information, write to the following organizations:

Superintendent of Documents
United States Government Printing Office
Washington D.C. 20402

U.S. Civil Service Commission
Washington D.C.20415

U.S. Department of Commerce
International Trade Administration
and Minority Business Development Agency
Washington D.C. 20025

U.S. Department of Labor
Bureau of Labor Statistics
Washington D.C. 20025

U.S. Department of Labor
Women's Bureau
Washington D.C. 20025

U.S. Department of the Interior
Division of Personnel Management
Washington D.C. 20025

Veterans Administration
Washington D.C. 20025

Small Business Administration
(See your telephone directory for nearest
regional office)

For information on occupational counseling and guidance for those
who are seeking personal help choosing a career, write to The
American Personnel and Guidance Association. It publishes a
"Directory of Approved Counseling Agencies" that lists places
where counseling services are available. The address of the
association is:

1607 New Hampshire Avenue NW
Washington D.C. 20009

CHAPTER XII

Electronic Learning

THOUGHT: The greatest challenge today is to become a better learner, using the advanced technology of our time.

The Author

The class of 2000 faces educational demands far beyond those of their parents. Will you be among those who will graduate around the turn of the century? If the answer is yes, you will need a better education simply to get a decent job. Most occupations in this country will require some skill with information-processing technology.

Your study skills and your ability to learn by using computer-aided programs must now go hand in hand. Educators are teaching with computers and software, with video recordings and telecommunication systems as well as with textbooks. So the way you study and learn must include the use of modern technology. Computers, robots, telecommunication, and videodiscs are learning tools that can be your window into the Information Age.

The author and social scientist Marvin J. Cetron has said, "... By the year 2030, when the class of 2000 will still be working, they will have had to assimilate more inventions and more new information than have appeared in the last 150 years."

Let's examine some high technology terms that you will need to know and discover what teaching/learning tools are available to fine-tune our study skills.

Computer-assisted Instruction

Computer-assisted instruction (CAI) refers to assignments done using a diskette (software program) and a computer. It enables you to become familiar with important information through drill and practice, simulation, problem-solving, and games. Your computer is programmed to ask and answer questions. A tutorial program can help you learn the goals, directions, special words, and strategies for accomplishing a given assignment using a computer program.

For instance, if you are learning a foreign language, memorizing math or science terms, or studying a list of spelling words, CAI programs can guide you step by step through the learning process. The computer may even play a game of Hangperson with you, using important vocabulary terms.

Suppose you are taking an English course in high school. Your teacher might organize the course into sections with objectives, drill and practice, and tests. The tutorial your teacher provides will help you understand the practice exercises, give you immediate feedback, and present the information in a more interesting fashion than your textbook does. Use of CAI will enhance study skills tenfold.

The use of a computer at home and in the classroom is the same: to control and manipulate ideas and information and to evaluate your progress in learning specific concepts. The advantage of home over classroom instruction is that you can work at your own pace. However, you may need a teacher to help you through an assignment or to explain directions that are new to you.

If you are a smart student and have learned and applied the study strategies in this book, your teacher may give you a software package that is advanced, stimulating, and entertaining. You can learn at your own pace, without feeling dumb or frustrated. It won't matter if you are behind, up with the class, or ahead of it. What will matter is your ability to develop study habits using a computer.

Simulations

Simulations are hypothetical problems or situations that help you further develop your problem-solving, thinking, and study skills. A "user-friendly" software program gives you data or basic information and interacts with you by giving you instructions and questions. You respond to questions and information on the screen or monitor of the computer. You can type in your answer using the keyboard or use a "mouse" device to point to something visual on the screen.

Learning was not always all fun and games. It still isn't. But simulations are challenging and as enjoyable as many adventure games. Programs like Oregon Trails, Odell Lake, and Flight

Simulator are designed to make you think, gather data, and make decisions based upon real events. They help you learn to concentrate, read for details, and learn fundamental concepts in a particular subject area.

Robots

Logo's Turtle, Onmibot, and Max Steele are only three of a growing number of robots that you may meet in your classes. They will help you better understand today's technology. You will learn to give and receive directions and to interact with machines as you solve problems, play games, and make decisions using simulations.

What do robots have to do with study strategies? They can store information. You can help a robot store, rearrange, and manipulate the data you want to use. Each one will remember your name, give you friendly feedback, be your learning partner, and perhaps more important, be very patient while you develop your study and critical thinking skills.

Telecommunication and Databases

In Chapter VIII we discussed the use of the library and how to gather information. Equally important is how to discover information through telecommunication. Using a computer, you can send and receive information over telephone lines. When you are stuck on a homework assignment, you can get help via computer from your friends, the library, and subscriber-supported services.

The SOURCE, MIX, COMPUSERVE, and GENIE are services that store a vast amount of information in their databases. They are a phone call away. They make information available to you for a minute-by-minute connection fee. You can do research for an essay in English, a report in History or Science, or almost any subject imaginable. You can also use your computer to call local bulletin board systems (BBS). Many of these are free services. They too have information about a variety of topics.

A database is a large body of electronically stored information. Government agencies, for example, use Census databases, Vital Statistics databases, Internal Revenue Service databases, and more. Many services contain volumes of information much like that found in encyclopedias. It you have a hobby, a sport, or special subject of interest, you may want to develop your own database for future reference. Using the technology available today, the possibilities for gathering and storing data are almost limitless.

Educational Resources Information Center

An important database service that you will want to become familiar with in your high school and college years is the Educational Resources Information Center (ERIC). It is available at most college and university libraries. The librarian will show you how easy this service has made library research. Instead of poring through ten or twenty magazines that you think might help you write an assigned report, ERIC locates timely information by scanning more than double that number. This database will not only save you time but will give you the most current facts and figures about your topic.

Compact Discs and Videodiscs

A system of computers, cameras, software programs, videodiscs, and high-resolution printers makes it easy to photograph, draw, and store images and retrieve data. You have already been exposed to some of this technology in your classroom. Your teachers are now showing more films designed from this type of system. In fact, students are learning to interact with compact disc (CD) and video-disc simulations much like the computer simulations previously mentioned. One disc may contain a complete electronic version of an encyclopedia. Instead of computer graphics, you get high-quality visual images and realistic sound and narration while you learn.

Using a combination of machines, computers, VCRs, CDs, and videodiscs, your teacher can introduce you to photographic images of art, historical events, scientific illustrations, experiments, and other subjects that you read about in your textbooks.

In the future, there will be more learning centers with smaller, more sophisticated computers and more powerful database systems. Some schools are already using artificial intelligence, speech synthesis, and advanced robotics. The computers of tomorrow will be used for business, personal, and social uses and, of course, for learning. Develop your ability to learn using our advanced technology.

EPILOGUE

The Ten Commandments of Study Strategy

1. ENJOY WHAT YOU STUDY
Study with enthusiasm and curiosity. Find a measure of self-satisfaction when you have gained some knowledge and have put it to use for the good of others as well as yourself. There is a great deal of enjoyment in overcoming ignorance, especially if you have a plan that meets the challenges and demands necessary for realizing personal goals and aspirations.

2. SHARE YOUR KNOWLEDGE
Man's thoughts and ideas were never meant to be locked up, kept secret, or hidden away from others. The most important characteristic of knowledge is that it eventually is shared, enlightening the pursuits of those who seek after it. And you become richer by far for sharing what you know with others, because in return you will discover even more.

3. FIND WHAT PROFITS YOU THE MOST
Choose those courses of action that will help you prosper. Develop a kaleidoscope of ideas from various learning experiences. Today, there is almost unlimited potential for increasing our happiness through awareness and knowledge.

4. STUDY ACTIVELY
Sharpen your sensitivities to new learning experiences that come your way. Observe, criticize, and evaluate continually. Divide and conquer the unknown as you learn to live with truth and wisdom.

5. ARRANGE A LEARNING ROUTINE IN YOUR LIFE
Consider the time you invest in learning. Put aside one or two hours per day to read, listen, and discuss matters that concern us all. Take the time to reflect upon matters that have value. Set aside other worries and concerns and free your mental abilities so you may ponder what ongoing relationship you have with reality. Relax and satisfy your curiosity on a regular basis.

6. ADAPT TO ANY LEARNING SITUATION

Develop your study skills to the point that noise does not disturb your learning experiences. In the beginning we need a quiet, comfortable place to learn. But as we master essential study skills, learning in various surroundings can be a new challenge. Constantly strive to learn more complex concepts, in less conducive surroundings. Take command of your reality and satisfy your intellectual nature whenever and wherever you feel most comfortable.

7. PRACTICE WHAT YOU LEARN

You will not find the surgeon who has diligently studied and developed painstaking skills not practicing his art in the operating room. Nor will you find an athlete who has trained and mastered skills in a sport not competing for recognition. Why, then, should we learn for the sake of learning without changing our habits and thinking accordingly?

8. PLAN FOR THE FUTURE

Unintelligent or unenergetic people usually procrastinate, learning very little late in life. Others plan for the future. They know the value of an education, and they realize that their future is worth looking after. More and more people are seeking ways to improve their way of living, because they also realize that time and change are inevitable. They learn to cope as they strive to meet future goals.

9. STUDY TO LEARN HOW TO LEARN

Keep up with modern-day technology, new ideas, theories, and innovation from all walks of life. Learning is an ongoing endeavor, the challenge to revitalize our awareness of reality and maintain our sense of integrity and happiness.

10. RESPECT YOURSELF AND YOUR ABILITY TO GROW
    IN KNOWLEDGE

Keep your mind active, your body healthy, and your brain stimulated by always being alert to new ideas. Keep a positive attitude as your old ideas are discarded and new knowledge becomes part of reality. Cherish those inner abilities to think, reason, make decisions independently, with creativity and intelligence. Know what you need to know in each stage of your life. Then, take full responsibility to study and learn.

STUDY STRATEGY is a lifelong plan for you to follow. It will take you to higher levels of learning, leaving you with an abundance of knowledge and satisfying memories.

NOW, ARE YOU READY TO MEET YOURSELF IN THE FUTURE?

Bibliography

Adams, W. Royce. *Reading Skills: A Guide to Better Reading*. John Witey & Sons, 1974.

Apps, Jerold W. *Study Skills for Adults Returning to School*. McGraw-Hill Book Co., 1978.

Armstrong, William H. *Study Is Hard Work*. Harper Brothers Publishers, 1956.

Beggs, David W. III and Edward G. Buffie. *Independent Study*. Indiana University Press, 1965.

Berman, Sanford I. *Understanding and Being Understood*. International Society for General Semantics, 1969.

Bitter, Gary G., and Ruth A. Camuse, *Using a Microcomputer in the Classroom*, Prentice-Hall, 1988.

Brilhart, John K. *Effective Group Discussion*. Wm. C. Brown Publishing, 1974.

Cannings, Terence R., and Stephen W. Brown. *The Information Age Classroom: Using the Computer as a Tool*, Franklin, Beedle & Associates, 1986.

Devine, Thomas G. *Teaching Study Skills*. Allyn and Bacon, Inc., 1981.

Einstein, Bernice W. *Guide to Success in College*. Grosset & Dunlap Publishers, 1967.

Elliot, H.C. *The Effective Student*. Harper & Row, Publishers, 1966.

Fedde, Norman A. *Preparing for College Study*. Readers Press, Inc., 1961.

Gulley, Halbert E. *Discussion, Conference, and Group Process*. Holt, Rinehart and Winston, Inc., 1968.

Joffe, Irwin L. *Finding Main Ideas*. Wadsworth Publishing Company, Inc., 1970.

Kai, Frederick S., and Eugene J. Kerstients. *Study-Reading for College Courses*. The Macmillan Co., 1968.

Langan, John. *English Skills*. McGraw-Hill Company, 1981.

Langdon, Grace, and Irving W. Stout. *Homework*. The John Day Company, 1969.

Mace, C.A. *The Psychology of Study*. Methuen & Co. Ltd., London, 1964.

Maddox, Harry. *How to Study.* Pan Books Ltd., London, 1932.
Main, Alex, *Encouraging Effective Learning.* Scottish Academic Press, Ltd., 1980.
Maxwell, Martha. *Improving Student Learning Skills.* Jossey-Bass Publishers, 1979.
Milan, Deanne K. *Developing College Skills.* Random House. 1983.
Pauk, Walter. *The Art of Learning.* Whittlesey House (McGraw-Hill), 1931.
Potter, David, and Martin P. Andersen. *Discussion: A Guide to Effective Practice.* Wadsworth Publishing Company. Inc., 1970.
Robinson, Francis. *Effective Study.* Harper Brothers, Publishers, 1961.
Salmon, Louis B. *Semantics and Common Sense.* Holt, Rinehart and Winston, Inc., 1966.
Samson, Richard W. *Problem-Solving Improvement.* McGraw-Hill Book Co., 1970.
Sanders, Donald H., *Computers Today*, McGraw-Hill, 1985.
Smith, Brenda D. *Bridging the Gap: College Reading.* Scott, Foresman Company, 1981.
Sumner, Mary, *Computers Concepts and Uses*, Prentice-Hall, 1985.
Tussing, Lyle. *Study and Succeed.* John Wiley and Sons, Inc., 1962.
Webster's New World Dictionary of the American Language. Simon and Schuster, 1982.

Index

history
  assignment, 37–38
  category, 85

I

ideas
  communicating, 114
  introductory, 70
  main, 35, 36, 63, 65, 68–69, 71,
    72, 75, 76
  organizing, 73
  summation of, 70
ignorance, overcoming, 26
illustration, 15, 73
imagination, 25, 28, 40
inductive writing, 76
information
  on assignments, 36, 62
  finding, 17, 22, 37
  gathering, 42, 75, 78, 83–91, 105
  giver/seeker, 109
  new vs. old. 5
  sources of, 85–86
informative statement, 2
initiator, discussion, 109
interrogative statement, 2
interview, 75, 85, 86–88, 90
introduction, 70, 71, 75

J

jargon, 52, 117–119
jobseeking, 114–122
journalistic writing, 77–78
judgment, standards of, 5, 40
judgmental questions, 40
Just-So Stories. The, 78

K

Kessleman-Turkel, Julie, 37–38
Kipling, Rudyard, 78
knowledge
  gaining, 92
  personal, 86

L

language
  category, 84
  command of, 47
  control of, 75
  as learning vehicle, 2, 92–94
  use of, 70
learning, 1–12, 25
  heuristic, 2
  improvement of, 19–23
  meaningful, 1, 2
  process, 92
  responsibility for, 2, 8, 20
  survey, 17–18
librarian, 4, 22, 37, 83, 88
library
  studying in, 17, 29
  use of, 83–85, 88–89, 125–126
listening
  active, 96–99
  vs. hearing, 13, 98
  in interviewing, 87
  learning by, 13–15
  vs. reading, 96
  to speech, 48–49
literature, 85
Locke, John, 4
log
  communication, 96
  listening, 100
  reading, 66

M

Maslow, Abraham, 32
mathematics, 28
  assignments, 36–37
meaning
  implied, 49–50
  word, 48, 54–55
memory, improving, 9
messages
  sending/receiving, 95, 96
  verbal, 98
misinformation, 8

oral, 102
short, 75–76
writing, 81–82
research, 41, 71, 75, 83
database, 125
resources
learning, 4, 17, 19, 22–23, 25
library, 21, 88–89
response, communication, 95–96
robots, 123, 125
Rogers, Will, 31–32
role-playing, 106
root, word, 48, 52, 57
rules
language, 93
memorizing, 36

S

saturation point, 20
scanning, 35–36, 37–38, 53, 61, 64
schedule, study, 2
science
assignments, 36–37
category, 84
self-actualization, 27–28
self-confidence, 71
self-contract, 33–34
sentence
function of, 3
understanding, 63
session, study, 8, 15–16, 17, 20,
35–36, 54
shoptalk, 48, 52, 117–119
simulation, 123, 124–125, 126
skill
communication, 92–104
job, 114–122
learning, 13–24
listening, 13–14, 97
reading, 60–69
research, 83
study, 3, 7, 8, 16, 22, 26, 114
vocabulary, 16–17
writing, 70–82
skimming, 15–16, 19, 20, 35–36,

37–38, 53, 61, 64
slang, 50, 93
social science, 84
social studies assignment, 37–38
software, 123, 124
spatial sequence, 71
speaking
as communication, 96
public, 42–43
speech, organizing, 102–103
speed-reading, 63, 64, 69
spelling, 47–48, 73, 76, 118
study
enjoyment of, 5–6
failure to, 5
group, 21, 105
place for, 29
Study Warm-Ups, 8–12, 20,
23–24, 32–34, 44–46, 57–59,
66–69, 80–82, 88–91, 99–104,
111–113, 119–122
subtopic, 16, 20
suffix, 48, 52
summarizing, 20, 72
survey, 75, 85, 86–88, 90
syllable, 54
symposium, 106
synonym, 48, 118
synthesizing questions, 39–40

T

teacher, 4, 22, 29, 37
clues from, 14
listening to, 97
technology, 84
information-processing, 123–126
telecommunication systems, 123,
125
terms
defining, 37–38, 73, 109
technical, 117–119
tests, studying for, 36, 65
thesaurus, 50
thinking
critical, 4–5